Praise for Carl Greer's previous award-winning books

Change Your Story, Change Your Life

Winner of a Beverly Hills Book Award, a Coalition of Visionary Resources Book Award, and an Indie Spiritual Book Award

"Engrossing"—**Lynn Andrews**, *New York Times* best-selling author of The Medicine Woman Series

"A wonderful and compassionate guide [linking] timeless ritual methods with modern active imaginal techniques. His clear explanations provide perspective, and his suggested exercises support personal exploration. A lovely book."—**Sylvia Brinton Perera**, LP, Jungian psychoanalyst, author of *Celtic Queen Maeve and Addiction*

"Can help anyone to break free of old agreements that no longer serve them and dream a new story."—**don Miguel Ruiz**, *New York Times* best-selling author of *The Four Agreements*

"….a rich guide to shedding old limiting stories and dreaming a new world into being."—**Alberto Villoldo**, PhD, *New York Times* best-selling author of *Shaman, Healer, Sage*

"Compelling . . . offers a brilliant synthesis of the tools of Jung's analytical psychology with . . . practices and rituals . . . [a] goldmine eminently accessible to the reader." —**Ashok Bedi, MD**, psychiatrist and Jungian analyst, author of *Path to the Soul* and *Crossing the Healing Zone*

"We were captivated …. {Greer} offers a way to take back self-mastery and once more become the director of our own lives . . . and create the world of our dreams."—**Jill Brierley and Sara Hollwey**, authors of *The Inner Camino: A Path of Awakening*

"Not only is he a wordsmith, but Greer is a wise Jungian . . . Those of us in need of change will learn to dance with archetypal energies and the transpersonal realms and work towards our personal healing and the healing of the world through our use of this book."—**Jessie Masterson, *Depth Insights***

"Much more than a 'quick fix' self-help book, containing a profound range of tools and exercises. Articulate and easily understandable, {the book} provides an excellent inspirational guide to personal transformation."—**June Kent, *Indie Shaman***

"informational and experiential"—***Somatic Psychotherapy Today***

Change the Story of Your Health

Winner of a Gold Nautilus Book Award, a Beverly Hills Book Award, a Best Book Awards award, and a Body, Mind Spirit Book Award in three categories

"**A tool for self-empowerment through knowledge and experience**"—*Somatic Psychotherapy Today*

"No matter what their health concern, **readers will find tools for writing and bringing to life a new health story**. Readers that begin using the practices on a regular basis will find it easier to let go of what is no longer serving them and bring in whatever can help them live according to a more satisfying health story."—*Natural Awakenings*

"Readers seeking to explore new ways to develop their inner calm, balance, self-love, and optimal physical health should find this approach **refreshing and full of possibilities. An appealing, helpful, and intriguing new approach to dealing with physical limitations and conditions.**"—*Kirkus Reviews*

"**For anyone looking for how to cope with health issues, including an accident or recent illness, *Change the Story of Your* Health is a valuable resource.** As a Jungian analyst, Carl Greer guides us how to unfold the power of our health story through journaling and expanded awareness practices to contact our 'inner healer.' . . . He encourages readers to 'write out the story of your health' which includes good habits, challenges, connections, partnering, family history, stress, goals, themes and concerns about mortality, and how to 'revise the story' as time passes, the body ages, or new health issues arise. He recommends using the expanded-awareness practice of dialoging in relationships and groups to help create a healing environment or community."—*Light of Consciousness*

"Carl Greer offers an interesting and original perspective on what it takes to be healthy and even to turn around states of ill health. . . . The first step is for the reader to understand what beliefs they have—their story—that might be determining their physical and emotional challenges and how they play out in their body and their health. To arrive at an understanding of what is going on under the surface of our conscious mind, Greer suggests a number of techniques, including meditation and journaling, as well as detailed questionnaires to lead the reader through an exploration of his or her own issues. The underlying message is that one first needs to understand how you got to where you are and then take responsibility for reframing your mind/story in order to open the way towards regaining your health. . . . Greer makes a very powerful case for the most important of these being one's beliefs."— *New Consciousness*

"In *Change the Story of Your Health*, clinical psychologist Carl Greer explains how to create a transformative health story using shamanic and Jungian techniques. The unconscious power of stories unlocks opportunities for healing as well as improved vitality, confidence, and stamina. 'Always remember that you are the storyteller,' writes Greer, 'and you do not have to live according to the dictates of a story written for you by your DNA, your past experiences and actions, or your cultural conditioning.' Greer recommends writing the story of your health by focusing on four health chapters or themes . . . Preparation is discussed, and journaling afterward to bring the story to life is recommended. Despite its use of alternative techniques, the book is practical, and is presented in a straightforward manner. Mini case studies show others' experiences with the energy exercises and the changes they made as a result. Greer makes clear that the intention of this work is to complement and enhance, not replace, western medicine. He recommends that clients check with a medical doctor as symptoms are uncovered, and he relates some of his own health challenges. Learning about the latest research, assistive devices, and medical interventions is encouraged. The work described here will take time, but **anyone interested in improving health challenges or who is curious about alternative healing techniques will find this to be an insightful guide.**"—Karen Ackland, *Foreword Reviews*

"*Change the Story of Your Health* discusses alternative medical traditions . . . and **comes from a clinical psychologist and Jungian analyst who has used these techniques, in conjunction with Western medicine, to help his own physical ailments and those of his clients.** . . The focus is on identifying blocks to health, more fully understanding one's current state of health and the keys to maintaining or improving it, and on applying journaling and dialoging techniques to expand self-awareness and tap inner resources for healing. . . . Readers determined to take charge of their path towards optimal health will find *Change the Story of Your Health* **contains a treasure trove of step-by-step processes** designed to lend insights into and modifications to overall health and approaches to life."—*California Bookwatch Midwest Book Review*

"*Change the Story of Your Health* offers a unique approach to self-exploration and healing. Drawing from traditional shamanism and Jungian principles, Greer captures the essence of connecting with nature and tapping into a greater spiritual awareness. Written in an **informative yet accessible** way, he reveals what he has learned on his health journey in the hopes that it will inspire and motivate others. Whether you're looking to maintain wellness as you age, manage a chronic illness or simply improve your overall well being, this book will guide you every step of the way. . . . Greer provides a fresh perspective . . . and **gives the reader practical tools they can apply to their everyday lives.**"—Rose Caiola, *Rewire Me*

"As a physician, I know all too well that many patients have health concerns due to inner factors that have not been addressed by conventional Western medicine. In *Change the Story of Your Health,* Dr. Greer **presents insightful self-healing measures from alternative medical traditions that will truly transform your personal health and well-being.**"—**Susan F. Reynolds, MD, PhD,** president and CEO, The Institute for Medical Leadership

"As an academic physician who has been on a journey of self-discovery for most of my life, I am delighted to find a work as clear and understandable as Carl Greer's *Change the Story of Your Health*. Dr. Greer has created **a remarkably accessible work offering fresh tools for self-exploration.** The writing is frank and clear, and it feels as if he is speaking directly to the reader. Carl's voice resonates in each sentence, conveying his deep integrity and desire to be of service to others. . . . The reader is offered approaches to self-discovery intended to provide insights into the profound life lessons offered to each of us through our health stories. This book is written for seekers who are searching for a fresh approach to self-understanding . . . While several of the exercises are drawn from age-old or traditional methods of communicating with one's inner teachers and guides, Dr. Greer has his own take on them, so they will feel new and personal to many. But, the reader must remember that the printed word is just the starting place—intentional application and some practice are needed to gain insights into the self and what lies behind one's personal health story. ***Change the Story of Your Health* is suitable for novice and experienced seekers alike.** Reading it and using its techniques can serve as a first step in changing our relationship to our lives and our health."—**David M. Steinhorn, MD**, professor of pediatrics, Children's National Health System, Washington, DC, medical director, Pediatric Palliative Care, and attending physician, Pediatric Intensive Care

"Accessible and compelling reflections on the ways in which the stories we tell ourselves about ourselves shape the lives we live. In today's world, Carl Greer's work **provides much-needed guidance for a more fulfilling and healthy way of life.**"—**George Hogenson, PhD,** Jungian analyst and author of *Jung's Struggle with Freud*

"**Carl Greer, PhD, PsyD, brings us another brilliant book,** helping us become aware of the story that impacts our health and rewrite it so that we achieve healing and well-being. In *Change the Story of Your Health,* Carl Greer shares a wealth of tools . . . **You will be inspired and feel motivated by the techniques he shares including journeying, dialoguing, chakra clearing, and engaging and partnering with earth, air, water, and fire to release old worn out-stories.** This book will open myriad possibilities for you to discover and work with your inner healer. I highly recommend *Change the Story of Your Health* for anyone who seeks to regain health and balance in our changing world."—**Sandra Ingerman, MA,** author of *Soul Retrieval* and *Walking in Light*

"*Change the Story of Your Health* **is beautifully written and a gem** for any reader who is looking to empower themselves, their health and their lives. We all have two general stories that we choose to live by: the story of our suffering and the story of our growth. You have the power to access your own story of growth and healing, should you choose. **Dr. Carl Greer weaves for you the wisdom of the healing traditions to provide you with the tools to create a new story of health, one that is full of love, healing and insight**. Read this book and change your story."—**Eva Selhub, MD**, author of *Your Health Destiny* and *Your Brain on Nature* and adjunct scientist in the neuroscience laboratory at the Jean Mayer USDA Human Nutrition Research Center on Aging at Tufts University (HNRCA)

The Necktie and the Jaguar

"Carl Greer has written **a moving testimonial to the reality of transformation in life's journey toward psychological and spiritual wholeness**. This narrative of his personal experience should be an **inspiration and encouragement** to others who find themselves also along the Way." —**Murray Stein, PhD**, Jungian analyst, past president of the International Association for Analytical Psychology and author of *Jung's Map of the Soul*

"Carl Greer is an explorer who clearly throws himself wholeheartedly into every angle of himself that he chooses to invest in. The result of his life search is this **powerful narrative**, which is a testament to his journey through the material, psychological and spiritual realms. Looking back on his eight decades on this planet, he has uncovered gold in unexpected places. This book **will offer insight and inspiration to its readers**." —**Malcolm Stern**, psychotherapist, author of *Slay Your Dragons with Compassion*, and cofounder of Alternatives

"Carl Greer's memoir of making radical changes in his life **shows that working with various states of consciousness can be extremely helpful in a creative process of personal transformation**. With journaling questions to support readers in their own self-reflection, *The Necktie and The Jaguar* **is an engaging story and a strong testament to the power of a mindful approach** to decision making, leadership, and living authentically." —**Ronald Alexander, PhD**, psychotherapist, author of *Core Creativity*

"Chronicling the seasons of a man's life—from child to sage, Carl Greer shares his remarkable journey as businessman, psychologist, Jungian analyst, shaman, and philanthropist, hence bridging the moral and the numinous on his path toward individuation. In reading his memoir, you get the real sense of being in the presence of a wise man with a fulfilled spiritual existence. His life story **will inspire you to become your possibilities and develop a deeper sense of grounding and purpose connected to something greater than ourselves**. What a truly extraordinary life."— **Jon Mills, PsyD, PhD, ABPP**, author of *The Mind-Body Problem*

"Providing at the end of each chapter many thought-provoking questions that are pegged to its themes, *The Necktie and the Jaguar* **encourages self-exploration and serves as a testament to the power of self-discovering, offering the reader insight and inspiration**. As Carl Greer learned, you don't have to feel trapped in a story someone else has written for you."—*California Bookwatch Midwest Book Review*

"A **compelling and cathartic** remembrance and self-help guide."—*Kirkus Reviews*

GO WITHIN TO CHANGE YOUR LIFE

A Hidden Wisdom Workbook for Personal Transformation

Carl Greer, PhD, PsyD

CHIRON PUBLICATIONS • ASHEVILLE, NORTH CAROLINA

www.ChironPublications.com

Cover design by Damian Keenan
Interior design by Danijela Mijailovic
Printed primarily in the United States of America.

ISBN 978-1-68503-535-8 paperback
ISBN 978-1-68503-536-5 hardcover
ISBN 978-1-68503-534-1 electronic
ISBN 978-1-68503-532-7 limited edition paperback
ISBN 978-1-68503-533-4 limited edition hardcover

Library of Congress Cataloging-in-Publication Data Pending

This book contains text from many of the blog pieces and articles Carl Greer has written over the years, which have appeared in publications and on his website and other websites, such as *OMTimes Magazine, Spirituality & Health Magazine, Natural Awakenings Magazine, Unity Magazine, Elephant Journal, The Edge Magazine, The Eden Magazine, InnerSelf Magazine, The Life Connection* magazine, *Creations Magazine, Whole Life Times, Essential Wellness* magazine, *Mantra Yoga + Health by Thrive, Wisdom Magazine, thirdAge,* and *Natural Solutions.* Carl Greer's poems in this book previously appeared in his book *Change Your Story, Change Your Life.*

Thanks to Alberto Villoldo, PhD, founder of The Four Winds Society, for permission to adapt his journeys to the lower and upper worlds and the rooms of contracts and treasures.

*To those who are willing to engage their hidden wisdom
and devote time to working with it to change their life story*

Acknowledgments

As a reader and writer of self-help books, I know that at one level, that of our minds and thoughts, it can be refreshing to gain new ideas. At another level, that of making a commitment of time and effort to change, I know many aren't willing to do the work required to make significant, lasting changes in the ways they approach and live their lives.

Since the publications of my three books—*Change Your Story, Change Your Life,* plus *Change the Story of Your Health* and *The Necktie and the Jaguar*—I have had some readers contact me and request more exercises and tools for transformation because they found the ones I shared to be very helpful. This workbook is in response to those requests. I believe that those willing to devote the time and effort to the practices described in this workbook can make lasting positive changes in their lives. These changes can stick because they come from you and your hidden wisdom, which knows best what you need and desire if you are to live with a sense of purpose, fulfillment, and contentment. Many exercises here will help you tap into your hidden wisdom.

In writing this workbook, I've had a number of people help me keep various areas of my life moving forward. In my day-to-day business and philanthropic endeavors, Lisa Sanchez and Don Waterlander have been helpful allies. My friend and doctor, Scott Kolbaba, has been there for me to discuss and strategize about my various health issues. Michael Doctorman, Lou Harrison, and Terry Robbins have been friends and advisors in my planning for succession "in the afterwards, when I am no longer here."

Nancy Peske, my intrepid editor and media and publishing consultant, has once again been a strong support as I have wrestled with the various drafts of this workbook. She did this in the midst of dealing with *suddenlies* in her own life during the creation of this book. Gail Torr and Colby Devitt have helped me get my work out into the world through their publicity, marketing, and social media skills.

I am thankful for my children and stepchildren, and their spouses, and my grandchildren, all of whom give me joy. Finally, my wife, Pat, was a source of love and inspiration for me as she battled terminal leukemia. Pat passed on August 15, 2024.

Contents

Introduction

You Have the Power to Change Your Life for the Better

You have the power to shape your experiences and live with greater authenticity, fulfillment, and purpose. As a retired Jungian analyst, clinical psychologist, and shamanic practitioner who helped clients over several decades, I know you have an extremely powerful resource: your hidden wisdom. You can call it your intuition, your inner voice, or something else, but however you think of it, your hidden wisdom has invaluable insights about you and your life. You can use what you learn from your hidden wisdom to make changes you say you want to make but for some reason never seem to. If you're feeling stuck and frustrated, this book will help.

In *Go Within to Change Your Life*, you'll find journaling exercises, guided visualizations, journeys, and other tools for accessing your hidden wisdom. All of these are designed to help you embrace change and dance elegantly with it as you set the foundation for an even better tomorrow. *Go Within to Change Your Life* will enable you to make use of resources you didn't know you had but were available to you all along. The insights and energy you gain can break you out of an old story that is no longer working for you, a story about your limitations and what you can't control or significantly affect.

This workbook starts with explanations of some of my core ideas about why people struggle to make changes they say they want to make: They get stuck in a *story*, influenced by unseen energies they don't realize they can engage and negotiate with so that these energies affect them differently. They also overlook their values and priorities, causing them to spend a lot of time on activities that don't bring them closer to the life they would like to live. They give up too easily when faced with obstacles because they don't know how to get around them. They set vague goals, but don't have a clear sense of how to reach them and don't hold themselves accountable for taking the small steps they need to take on a new path. They get demoralized by losses, failures, and disappointments, and become afraid their options are limited. All these challenges will be easier to tackle once you've read and worked with *Go Within to Change Your Life*.

I understand what it feels like to be restless yet unsure of what I wanted to create for myself. I know what it's like to feel you're stuck in a story written by someone else—your family, your community—and wondering how to break out of it. I was a successful businessman with a wife, kids, home, and good job, but it wasn't enough for me. I dared to dream of something different, of pursuing my interest in psychology, and began on a long period of training to become a licensed clinical psychologist and then, a Jungian analyst. Simultaneously, I continued my study of martial arts, which helped me learn valuable lessons about conflict that I applied in business and my personal life. And when I was in my late 50s, I began studying shamanism, eventually becoming a shamanic practitioner, teacher, and workshop leader.

Back when I was feeling that I was living life robotically, without a sense of vitality, I could not have imagined where I am today. I have spent the past decade or so sharing through books and articles what I have learned from my experiences, which include changing my career, becoming a Jungian analyst, and studying and teaching shamanic practices. The feedback I've gotten is that the ideas and exercises I shared have helped people lead better lives and even experience significant changes. The questions I've asked them to ponder have assisted them in their personal growth. Because of that feedback, I decided to create this workbook, hoping people will do more than just read about the ideas and instead, use the exercises to begin to experience changes they say they want to make. The journaling questions you'll find throughout this workbook are likely to be of even greater value if you use some of the hidden-wisdom techniques in this book alongside them. To do the hidden-wisdom exercises, you must enter a meditative state. That way, you won't be distracted by your usual biases and ways of thinking. You might be surprised by what you can achieve by consciously planning an interaction with your unconscious while also being open to any surprises it might have for you.

Please know that you do *not* have to do all the exercises to benefit from this workbook. I wanted to make sure you had a wide variety to choose from. If in reading and working with this book it feels that I'm asking you the same things in different ways, it's because I'm trying to give you more than one doorway to understanding your story so you're better able to change it if it's not a satisfying one. If you're thinking of skipping an exercise because it seems you've done a similar one, keep that in mind.

Before I retired, when clients came to me as a Jungian analyst and clinical psychologist to seek help with transformation, I customized my approach for each individual. I don't want to impose rules on you about how to use this book. You can decide whether to approach the work methodically and set specific goals, such as doing one or two sections every weekend. You could start with chapters 1 and 2 and continue through the entire book in a linear fashion, or you might let your intuition guide you as to which chapters and exercises to focus on after you have completed the foundational work in part 1. However, I strongly encourage you to try several *types* of exercises you'll find here and don't rush through them. Some might seem to be straightforward, easy journaling exercises, but it's important to take your time with them and self-reflect before you answer so you get the most out of them.

You do NOT need to do all the exercises in this book to start feeling a shift and seeing personal transformation. Feel free to customize your approach to this workbook, letting your intuition guide you. I strongly encourage you to try several types of exercises in this book.

If you find you aren't doing the work of this book, I suggest you set up a schedule for it or alter the schedule you created. You could even decide to use a hidden-wisdom technique to learn more about why you may be resisting the work you say you want to do. Chapter 9: *If You're Not Meeting Your Goals* might be very helpful if you find yourself stalled out on the way to your goals and have started to abandon this workbook because you aren't making changes you were hoping to make. I've often found that when the work of transformation starts to feel laborious, so much so that a person is tempted to quit, a breakthrough occurs. I encourage you to trust in the process of using this workbook as a guide for personal transformation.

The more you put into the work of this book, the more you'll get out of it. I'm confident that if you dedicate yourself to reading the material and doing the exercises, many of which require you to access your hidden wisdom using techniques you'll learn along the way, you'll gain valuable information about yourself that you might not have encountered had you not done the work. What you choose to do with that information and any energies you draw in that can help you make changes is up to you.

Also, it might be easier to hold yourself accountable for doing the work in this book if you find others willing to do the work as well—for example if you are in a book group or a group dedicated to enhancing wellness or spirituality. If you do work with others, be respectful of each other's confidentiality. Set up some rules for sharing insights with others in the group and commenting on their experiences, and celebrate each other's breakthroughs and newfound insights.

Whether you work with the book alone or with others, remember that you can't change other people, but you can change yourself. You can alter how you look at relationships, how you think about yourself, how you act in various situations, how you respond to conflict, and so on. Regardless of how much of this workbook you end up completing, or what your personal approach to using it is, it can help you gain important information about what's preventing you from having the kinds of experiences you want and how to rid yourself of any obstacles standing in your way. Additionally, you will learn much about yourself and find it easier to believe you can achieve personal transformation. I hope you'll make a point of coming back to it again and again over time to deepen your self-understanding and make use of its tools for transformation. I wish you the best as you begin your exploration of your hidden wisdom.

While you can't change other people, you can change yourself.

How This Book Is Structured to Support Your Transformation

In part 1 of this book, you'll learn about your hidden wisdom and how to access and interact with it—and with archetypal energies that reside in the unconscious. You will learn about these energies and discover hidden-wisdom exercises for accessing them and gaining insights and momentum for transformation from them. You'll also start to identify a story about your life that's influencing you without your awareness (most people have such a story). You'll examine that old story, decide what you might change it to, and consciously write a new, more satisfying story. You can work with this story throughout the book, using hidden-wisdom techniques to figure out how you'd like to change it so you can consciously write a new and better story and bring it to life. You can continue to journal and use hidden-wisdom techniques as you start to set goals and make changes that align with this new, more satisfying story. If you've been frustrated in the past by your inability to make new habits stick, I think you'll be excited to find that with the help of your hidden wisdom, that work will be much easier. You'll find you're better able to identify obstacles to your goals and ways to overcome those roadblocks.

Whenever you encounter the target icon in this book (you'll come across it initially in Chapter 5: *Your Story and How You Can Change It*), you'll have a chance to set a specific goal that includes a time frame for achieving it, so you'll hold yourself accountable. I also suggest you record in your calendar two or three checkpoints for progressing toward your goal. Setting goals helps ensure that you take action to apply lessons from your hidden wisdom to your life and actually make changes. Goals don't have to be grand. They can be as simple as being less reactive to other people's behavior or being more focused on your health. What goals you set is entirely up to you.

In part 1, you will learn how to start working with dreams, guided visualizations, and journeys and discover your wise inner self. All these can expose your conscious mind to hidden wisdom.

When you encounter the target icon in this book, you'll have a chance to set a specific goal that includes a time frame for achieving it, so you'll hold yourself accountable.

In part 2, you'll begin applying what you've learned as a result of the work you'll have done so far. Internal transformation is important, but you also have to change your behaviors. In part 2, you may want to skip around to work with the chapters that most appeal to you.

In Chapter 6, you'll identify your values and priorities, which will help you set more goals that are right for you. It's easier to stick with a goal if you've set it for the right reasons, but sometimes we feel we have to live in alignment with a story someone else wrote for us, playing a particular role, so we pursue goals that aren't in synch with our values. Sometimes, the biggest obstacle to achieving our goal is that the goal doesn't truly mesh with our values and priorities, which causes us to unconsciously sabotage our progress. Doing the exercises and reading the related material will make it easier to discover any stumbling blocks and how to overcome them.

In Chapter 7, you'll learn to become more mindful and observant. Self-reflection will help you immensely as you work toward personal transformation. Very often, we say we want to change but don't because deep down, there's a part of us that's resistant.

Chapter 8 will have you setting and achieving more goals so you can take wise action, applying what you learned using hidden-wisdom techniques so that you achieve the changes you seek. Insights can be inspiring, but if you genuinely seek change, you have to set goals for making that happen and learn how to be accountable to yourself.

Chapter 9: *If You're Not Meeting Your Goals* helps you reflect on your progress so far. You'll get help in identifying any obstacles to attaining your goals and living according to your new story. Knowing what's holding you back, you can get unstuck. You can make some new choices and take some new actions. You might find yourself consciously abandoning a goal, changing it, or overcoming an obstacle that you never realized was blocking you.

Chapter 10 teaches you how to resolve conflicts, drawing on hidden wisdom and the momentum you've established for transformation. Conflicts in relationships with others are inevitable, but you can learn to tolerate any discomfort associated with them and use conflicts as opportunities to deepen your trust and intimacy with others while also being true to yourself and your values and goals.

If you've been limiting your aspirations, Chapter 11: *Create the Life You Desire* will help you dream a bigger dream. It's a good chapter to check out if you're clear on some of the things in your life that aren't working for you but unsure of what you would like to replace them.

Chapter 12: *Resilience When Presented with Life's Suddenlies* will help you let go of fear as you adjust to unexpected changes in your life. Chapter 13 will guide you in transforming your relationship with *Source* (my term for God or Spirit) and nature, while Chapter 14 focuses on changes related to your health. Chapter 15 will help you with the difficult task of contemplating endings you recognize you may not be able to avoid—including your death or that of someone you care about deeply.

Again, feel free to customize your approach to the book. Give yourself credit for the work you do, and reflect on how it is helping you. I believe that doing so will keep you motivated in using this tool for transformation.

Part I
Learn to Access Your Hidden Wisdom and Its Treasures

Chapter 1
The Secret to Hidden Wisdom Within You

"Our remedies oft in ourselves do lie, Which we ascribe to Heaven."

—William Shakespeare, *All's Well That Ends Well*

Do you resist the idea that you can make your life better? Are you quick to look outside yourself for someone to rescue or fix you? You might be underestimating the transformative power of your own hidden wisdom, which lies within.

Hidden wisdom has been called wisdom and insights from the unconscious or even the *collective unconscious*, the unconscious we all share, according to Carl Jung. It has also been called "that small inner voice." Regardless of your beliefs about where this wisdom originates, it is authentic, offering valuable insights that can help you reflect on what changes you'd like to make, why you'd like to make them, and how you can go about transformation.

All of us have attitudes that are ingrained within us and hard to change—for example, we might have beliefs such as, *You have to assume people are untrustworthy* or *That's just how things work—I have to accept my powerlessness.* This book is about going within and working with your hidden wisdom to access ideas and resources for changing situations that may seem impossible to transform. You'll learn you have more freedom than you think—including the freedom to transform what may seem unchangeable. Altering your attitude alone might greatly increase your sense of happiness and fulfillment, making it easier for you to overcome fear, cynicism, and pessimism.

I worked for several decades as a clinical psychologist and Jungian analyst, shamanic practitioner (a healer who works with energy), and workshop leader. These experiences taught me that while some people say they want to change, very often, some part of them is resistant. I have guided hundreds of people into using techniques for tapping into their hidden wisdom, including journaling, dialoguing, dreamwork, visualizing, journeying, and making nature paintings. These techniques can yield valuable insights. From there, it's easier to change—or to confidently and consciously decide to find ways to be happier and more at peace with your current situation.

That's because the techniques help you perceive your circumstances differently and recognize your capacity for personal transformation. Accessing your hidden wisdom can inspire new goals and new ideas for how you want to live.

My work with others, along with my spiritual studies and practices, has taught me that often, when people experience breakthroughs and reinvigorated determination to move forward, they experience an energetic shift. It can seem that your life's experiences are dictated by fate, a powerful force that you can't direct. But in my experience, by working with your hidden wisdom, which is in the unconscious, you can alter energetic influences on you that you might not even realize exist. You can make them work for you instead of against you. The hidden-wisdom techniques will be an essential tool for this work of going within to change your life.

Hidden wisdom is inside all of us. I believe this wisdom is sourced from Spirit or God, which is why I call this loving higher power Source. However, you can use any term that makes you comfortable. I've used both "Source" and "Spirit" throughout this book.

In my experience, Source's nature is to love us unconditionally, and Source collaborates with us to create the lives we long to lead. If you don't believe in a higher power, that's okay. You can still benefit from the exercises you'll find here, which will teach you how to go within, beyond the limits of your conscious mind, to gain insights and even energy for transformation.

The hidden energetic influences I speak of are what I call archetypal energies. They are embodied in familiar characters and depicted in stories well known to most people. An archetype is an original model or representation—like the fool, the warrior, or the rebel. Archetypal energies' influence on us can keep us stuck in unpleasant situations and drawn to familiar ones even though we may have vowed, *I'll never get into a situation like that again!* If we have hidden resistance to changes we long to make, we need to become aware of that resistance and work with it consciously. Otherwise, archetypal energies will continue to draw us back into our old patterns regardless of how much we might protest that we truly want to change. We'll get stuck being the lone wolf, the stern taskmaster, and so on.

The stories we're living, according to the patterns we find ourselves trapped in, may not be ones we are aware of having chosen. Often, they were written for us by our families and communities, so it's common for our stories to be out of synch with what we most hope to experience. Your hidden wisdom can help you recognize old stories that are no longer working for you and discard them. Then, you can become the storyteller in your life and free yourself from the constriction of the old story.

It's good to consciously discipline yourself to make one small change after another that can add up to a big transformation. This workbook gives you some guidance on how to make what I call *small changes around the margins*. However, you'll also want to use tools for change that are too often overlooked: Techniques for accessing, learning from, and even negotiating with archetypal energies that are influencing you. You can do all of this by getting in touch with your unconscious mind, which is where hidden wisdom resides and where you can connect with archetypal energies.

Overcoming Any Fear

One way the archetypal energies you'll encounter can help you avoid returning to old patterns that were a problem is by challenging your fears. Fear of the unknown is one of the biggest obstacles to change. There's a certain comfort to familiarity. Better the hell you know than the one you don't know, as the saying goes. But you don't have to experience hell—you can learn to become more comfortable with change and unfamiliar experiences.

Asserting yourself, setting healthy boundaries with other people, and saying *no* to activities that don't serve you will feel awkward at first. You might worry about how people respond to your new ways of interacting. Working with your hidden wisdom, you can learn to tolerate that discomfort as you make positive changes you want to make.

Also, you don't have to fear tapping into your unconscious to find the wisdom hidden there. In fact, if you never face what's in your unconscious, it's likely to have great influence on your life—influence that can cause all sorts of problems. Of course, some people have repressed trauma. If that's the case, or you suspect it is, I encourage you to work with a therapist, counselor, or analyst while using this book and to put it down when you're uncomfortable, checking in with yourself to decide whether to seek professional help before continuing.

You will be doing journeys, which are like guided visualizations, and whenever you journey, you'll be instructed to encounter a guardian who must grant you permission before you go further into working with your unconscious. The purpose of this guardian is to provide you with psychological protection against a too-intense experience of recalling memories. Is the guardian real? Some might say it's an expression of Source (God) protecting you—or a protective aspect of your own consciousness. You can decide what you believe.

Encountering and Engaging Energies

When you use some of the exercises, you'll imagine yourself traveling into the future or to a room of treasures where you can claim gifts that can help you in your quest for personal transformation. These gifts can be insights but also energies. Let's say you encounter the insight that you need to be less hard on yourself, and it's accompanied by the energy of self-compassion. The insight and energy can help you by altering how you interact with others and showing you that you may be undervaluing your contribution to a relationship and being too hard on yourself.

Using the hidden-wisdom techniques, you'll work with symbols, figures, or energies through *dialoguing*. Dialoguing is a practice for learning from and negotiating with what's in your unconscious. You have a conversation with a symbol or figure from a dream or with an emotion, your resistance to change, or your wise inner self, to give a few examples. Keep in mind that you can end the dialogue any time you feel uneasy and, if you like, come back another time when you're more prepared to learn from it. For example, you might learn through a dialogue that you're not being honest with yourself about how much you are giving to others out of your own needs instead of theirs and that you're sometimes upsetting people with your behavior. This insight might embarrass you. I encourage you to stay with the dialogues and hidden-wisdom techniques even if you find them emotionally challenging. They can be extremely powerful for transformation.

As I said in the Introduction, if you work with the hidden-wisdom exercises (which there are many of in this book), you'll get even more out of the journaling ones. Use both types of exercises together for the greatest benefit—and be sure you hold yourself accountable for making changes in your life, even in small ways. (You'll read more about how to do that in part 2.)

You will be working with your hidden wisdom and archetypal energies while in a meditative state, with your analytical mind's busy activity quieted enough for you to not be distracted by your usual biases and ways of thinking. You'll learn about becoming quiet and going within with a plan for what you want to do while in a non-ordinary state of consciousness. Consciously plan an interaction with your unconscious while also being open to any unexpected experiences it might inspire—and then, see what happens.

You will be working with your hidden wisdom and archetypal energies while in a meditative state.

Stories and Archetypal Energies

Stories strongly influence us. You don't have to live according to a destiny determined by your past. In this workbook, you'll find exercises for identifying your story—not the one you'd like to believe you're living according to but the one that is actually shaping your perceptions *and* your experiences. Its energetic influence on you is powerful, and by working with your hidden wisdom, you can transform it to serve you better.

You might not be aware of your story. You may have trouble identifying it at first. Once you do, you may find that you don't like what you discover. However, you can use the exercises here to change your story, working with your wisdom that lies beyond the reach of your rational mind.

Archetypal energies' influence on us can keep us stuck in our stories and in unpleasant relationships and painful situations that feel familiar because they're in synch with our old story. They can also direct us toward people whose own patterns mirror or match ours. You may recognize these patterns and even have vowed never to fall back into them again.

Here are some common stories that can be hidden from a person's conscious awareness:

- People in my family all seem to die before they turn fifty, and that will probably happen to me, too, so why not just enjoy life and not worry about my health?

- I'm a lone cowboy, sometimes connecting with others but moving on before I feel tied down.

- I have to earn love through giving and giving because I'm not worthy of being loved as I am.

Can you see how such stories lying hidden in your unconscious mind could hold you back from achieving what you desire? You'll soon get a chance to think more deeply about what your story may be and whether it's working for you.

On Being Pushed Out of Your Comfort Zone

Time spent in contemplation and self-discovery can be pleasant or uncomfortable. Even when doing hidden-wisdom work and engaging archetypal energies is challenging or unpleasant, it's worth tolerating any discomfort so you can discover what your conscious mind is avoiding. You might need to explore your emotions or acknowledge hidden truths that make you uneasy. Discomfort is often part of growth. Deep down, you have a wise inner self that knows your deepest yearnings and how you get in your own way when trying to achieve your goals. This wise inner self doesn't want you to suffer unnecessarily. Its goal is to see you make changes that will lead to a greater sense of authenticity, fulfillment, and purpose, so it will give you access to your hidden wisdom.

If you tend to distract yourself from feelings and thoughts that upset you, you may be underestimating how much energy and courage you have to face your challenges and overestimating how unpleasant the work will be. Discovering and coming to understand the aspects of yourself and your life that cause you to be unhappy makes it easier to begin the process of change. Transformation can help you live with more satisfaction and a greater sense of control over your story. When you have conversations with your unconscious, seeking hidden wisdom, you begin to develop confidence in your ability to continue learning about yourself and applying your insights to your everyday life, improving it in myriad ways. The changes you say you're seeking will stop being so elusive. Gaining practice working with your hidden wisdom will lead you to eagerly engage this aspect of you because you have discovered how very helpful it can be. Don't be afraid to step out of your comfort zone and go within to gather insights and energy for transformation.

Take time to discover and understand the aspects of yourself and your life that make you unhappy. Then, you'll likely find it easier to begin to make important changes and live with more satisfaction and a greater sense of control over your story.

You Have More Power to Change Than You Think

Therapy patients are more likely to have successful outcomes when they see therapy as a tool for self-healing. Good physicians will ask their patients about their habits of mind and body and guide them to heal themselves through better lifestyle choices. Still, many of us continue to look outside ourselves for healing what is hurting us and standing in the way of a better life. We don't trust in our abilities to access the power or wisdom we need to cure what ails us.

Healers such as analysts, therapists, shamans, acupuncturists, and physicians don't have magical abilities. What they have are skills for helping people to help themselves. Using *Go Within to Change Your Life,* you can begin a process of developing a deeper awareness about yourself and your experiences. Then it will be easier to change your story and live according to a new one.

If you're afraid you don't have the time, energy, or resources to make changes in your life, be assured that if you work with the practices in this book, you will free up energy you're currently using to block your awareness of how dissatisfied you are.

We tend to rewrite our stories again and again. You can always write a new story, one that doesn't have to be a mere daydream or wishful thinking. You can bring it from dream to reality. You can do this by working with archetypal energies available to you when you consult your unconscious, using your hidden wisdom to guide and support you in your transformation.

Finally, you can't only change your thoughts or perceptions and expect transformation to happen as a result. You have to change your behavior and your energy. The mental shift can be the first step in making changes, and an energy shift will help you with transformation, but you must take new actions too.

Chapter 2
Meet the Archetypal Energies You'll Engage

Each of us has a life story, but we might not know what its themes are or what hidden beliefs drive our perceptions and responses to people and situations. In my experience, if we can discover what our true story is—not the one we tell others but the one that we genuinely believe deep down—we can change it and thereby change our lives.

Carl Jung believed that the stories of our lives are fueled by archetypal energies that exist in our shared collective unconscious and show up repeatedly in stories humans around the world share. We're all familiar with certain characters or plots that are part of mythology: The mischievous being who frustrates someone until that person realizes that they have some learning or growth to do. The star-crossed lovers who seem doomed to be kept apart. The self-sacrificing martyr who turns resentful and begins to manipulate others into doing their bidding. Often, we're drawn to myths, movies, and novels whose characters and plots remind us of how certain archetypal energies or energetic patterns play out in our own lives. They resonate for us because of experiences we've had or that we think, fear, or hope we might have some day. Archetypal energies can manifest as habits of mind, activity, or emotion or as roles we play.

Many people believe that all consciousness exists within the mind of a god who wants to help us. Connecting with your hidden wisdom and communicating with it might be a form of prayer or meditation for you, one that allows you to work with archetypes created by Source. (My own feeling is that the loving being many call God wants us to ask for help with our challenges, and that we can do that through prayer or consulting our hidden wisdom, which is always connected to Source and Source's wisdom and healing abilities.)

Think about a few of your favorite myths, movies, or novels—or ones that strongly affected you or perhaps even upset you. Write their titles and the simple plots below if you like, as doing so can help you better understand yourself. You can sum up the plots in a sentence or two—for example, *When (this) happens to (type of character), there's a problem: (name the problem). It's not until (fill in the blank) happens that (fill in the result/what changes).*

Myth/movie/novel #1 _____

_____

_____

_____

Myth/movie/novel #2 _____

_____

_____

_____

Myth/movie/novel #3 _____

_____

_____

_____

Often, we're drawn to myths, movies, and novels whose characters and plots remind us of how certain archetypal energies or energetic patterns play out in our own lives.

Strong feelings such as anger or shame can arise quickly and fiercely in the seemingly inoffensive situation of watching a movie. When that happens, it might indicate an archetype's influence on your life. For example, you might be especially upset by a character who is self-centered or betrays others. As you start to think about stories that speak to you, pay attention to:

- any themes you identify as being especially meaningful, intriguing, or emotionally affecting for you

- any themes that particularly bother you

- any characters that you feel are similar to you

- any characters you wish you were more like

- any characters you strongly dislike

You might want to fill in the following so you can better understand archetypal themes and characters that are likely to be affecting you in some way.

I seem to be drawn to stories with these themes: _____

_____

_____

_____

I don't like stories with these themes: _____

_____

_____

_____

Next, answer the following.

With which characters or types of characters do you identify? _____

_____

_____

Which characters or types of characters do you like? _____

_____

_____

Which characters or types of characters do you dislike? _____

_____

_____

Can you see any connection between characters and themes in movies and your life, and if so, what are they? _____

This exercise will help you identify your story. Again, your story is not necessarily the one you tell others about yourself and your life. It's the one that deep down, you believe to be true. You might be keeping it hidden from others and even yourself because it makes you feel vulnerable.

So, what is your story? Maybe it's a familiar plot that you've seen played out in movies and books. You can start by writing it out in two or three paragraphs and then summarizing it according to its theme and characters. For example, it might be:

- I work hard but no one really notices or appreciates it, so I feel invisible and even unimportant.

- I've let fear push me to focus on security instead of my creativity and my dreams. That's helped me support my family but made me feel like I always have to be a reliable provider and caretaker who never gets my moment to shine.

- I'm a dreamer and maybe a fool, too, because I didn't stick with my dreams and I'm not happy or contented with where I ended up.

- I've accomplished a lot in my life, but I'm not sure whether it's really me that made it all happen. Maybe I'm just lucky, and I don't really deserve my success.

- I can't count on anyone but myself. I'm a lone wolf, as independent as can be.

- I never seem to fit in, but I kind of like that about myself while also feeling sad that many people have rejected me or don't really accept me because I'm different.

In other words, what is your core belief about your life? If you're not sure what it is yet, don't worry. It may become clearer as you do the work in this book, and you might realize your story isn't what you thought it was initially. You'll get another chance to try to identify your story.

The story of my life is: _____

_____

_____

_____

_____

_____

_____

_____

_____

_____

_____

_____

Which Archetypal Energies Are Affecting You?

Let me share a little of my story so you can better understand the role of archetypal energies in shaping our life stories.

The energy of the hardworking Everyday Person determined my choices and experiences for many years: I grew up in the postwar Midwest, and my family and community seemed to want me to be a good student, go into business, and become a success as they defined it. I yearned to be more adventurous, to explore the big questions of life and perhaps find the poet within, but I felt pressured to be practical. The Everyday Person is one of the archetypes: It is the ordinary fellow who does what's expected of him, doesn't stand out from the crowd, and continues along a predetermined path in a predictable way, not contemplating his life.

Archetypes can express themselves in both positive and negative ways. For example, while the Everyday Person archetype kept me from listening to my inner call to adventure, it also helped me to succeed in business as well as to feel comfortable talking with a wide variety of people. You can influence how archetypes influence you and how much they do but only if you work with the archetypes consciously, so let's look more closely at some archetypes and their effects on you.

Think about whether you feel like the Everyday Person—or whether there's an Everyday Person in a novel, movie, or TV show that's familiar to you. You might have strong feelings about the Everyday Person—especially if this energy seems to be affecting you or someone you know. For example, maybe you dislike being seen as ordinary because it makes you feel you're boring and not worthy of the attention of interesting people. Maybe you worry that you are seen that way, so you feel uncomfortable seeing someone who behaves like an Everyday Person. You can record your thoughts and feelings about the Everyday Person and the Adventurer below.

My thoughts and feelings about the Everyday Person in my life: _____

_____

_____

_____

When I was younger and acting out the role of Everyday Person, there was another archetypal energy affecting my story. Its force wasn't as strong then as that of the Everyday Person, but the energy of the Adventurer was influencing me nonetheless. I longed to travel not just to other places but to experience firsthand what I had only read about in books.

I had a mythopoetic self: a part of me that very much wanted to know what it was like to feel at one with God or Spirit. I wanted to explore the mysteries of love, death, and the mind. I read books on psychology and spirituality, attended church, and practiced martial arts and qigong, which are spiritual disciplines. I was tapping into a spiritual Adventurer within myself.

As my Adventurer energy grew stronger, I felt increasingly restless. I needed to write a new story for myself. I needed to have the Everyday Person stop influencing me so strongly—to work more consciously with the Adventurer within, drawing on its strength to give me the courage to step off the old path. As daunting as it was at age forty-five to begin studying to become a clinical psychologist, then Jungian analyst, and then shamanic practitioner, which became my eventual adventurous goal, I started part-time. Had I known it would take me thirteen years of schooling and the remainder of a lifetime to reach my aim, I might have given up. Fortunately, my Adventurer energy had grown strong, and I credit it for helping me move forward with momentum. Eventually, my Adventurer energy would lead me to do more spiritual exploration, which led to my feeling even more satisfied with my life.

What about you? How as the Adventurer energy affected you?

My thoughts and feelings about the Adventurer in my life: _____

_____

_____

_____

Multiple Archetypes Can Affect You

The Everyday Person archetype still influences my story to some degree: I continue to live in the Midwest and to enjoy ordinary family life. I am still involved in business, which took up a lot of my time when the Everyday Person was dominating my story, but now I'm turning more of my energy to writing and philanthropy. Today, the Everyday Person dances with the Adventurer within me, joined by another energy, the Healer, who wants to help others do the soul work of changing their stories and changing their lives.

What about the Healer in your life? Maybe you can identify a time when the energy of healing, or a healer who had strong healing powers, helped you when you needed healing—or didn't help you when you needed assistance.

My thoughts and feelings about the Healer in my life: _____

_____

_____

_____

Archetypal patterns have always been enacted by other humans, but your experience of them can differ from that of others because you're a unique person. You might experience the archetype of the Fool as a playful clown who encourages you to take life less seriously—or as an energy of naïveté and gullibility. The same archetype might be experienced by someone else as a cunning and sophisticated court jester who dances on the edge of danger by revealing truth through humor. The Fool might be preventing you from having better relationships because it's causing you to use humor to avoid serious discussions your partner wants to have with you.

In working with your unconscious, you can try to access a particular archetype, whether it's one that's problematic for you or one that appeals to you. You can call on any archetype to help you understand your relationship with it. When you engage an archetype, you may find it can make an invaluable contribution to the new and better story you would like to write for yourself and bring to life.

Remember, archetypes can affect you positively or negatively. Maybe you succeeded in battling a disease by allowing the warrior archetype to influence you. On the other hand, you may be a warrior who didn't realize that you had an Achilles' heel that made you vulnerable, so as tough as you were, you experienced a tragedy.

The Changing Influence of Multiple Archetypal Energies

As you think about your own story in new ways, which you'll do while working with this book, you'll start identifying some archetypal energies that have influenced you and ones that you haven't thought were there for you all the time, ready to fuel your dreams. Below is a list of some archetypes, which you can also think of as roles you play in your life. You might want to circle the ones that you feel are influencing you, and, after the list in the space provided, explain where in your life you're seeing that archetype's influence. For example, if you circle the Leader, you might write: *In many aspects of my life, I'm the one asked to make decisions and plan what happens next. Sometimes that feels very burdensome, and I'd like others to take the lead occasionally so I can just be a follower.* Or you might write, *I've often been disappointed by leaders, but I don't feel I have what it takes to be a good leader, so I tolerate ineffective leaders. I'd like to discover whether I could be a good leader, however.*

Your story about a particular archetype might be one you tell yourself to make sense of the experiences you've had to this point. Your story of your life can lock you out of having different types of experiences and into having ones that are familiar—because you're operating according to old beliefs that are hidden in your unconscious.

You can reflect on the following archetypes and how they apply to you as you did with the Everyday Person, the Adventurer, and the Healer. I suggest you choose three archetypes you feel have had the most influence on your life, circle them, and explore them using the journaling exercises at the end of this list.

I've deliberately not defined each archetype because, as you learned earlier, we can all experience them in different ways. As you go over this list, you might close your eyes and imagine an example of each of these archetypes. That can help you identify how any particular archetype can be expressed. Also, remember that archetypes are energies. The Parent doesn't have to show up as a literal parent. You might have felt parental toward a younger person even if you were never a parent yourself.

The Everyday Person or Ordinary One

The Adventurer or Risk-Taking One

The Healer or Caretaking One

The Fool or Playful and Naïve One

The Sage or Wise One

The Leader or Authority Figure

The Spiritual or Mystic One

The Child or Innocent One

The Parent or Guide

The Lover or Romancer

The Rebel or Agitator

The Hero/Heroine or Rescuer

The Student or Novice

The Teacher or Mentor

The Artist or Innovator

The three archetypes I most identify with are: _____

_____

_____

_____

My thoughts and feelings about the first of those archetypes: _____

_____

_____

_____

My thoughts and feelings about the second of the archetypes I circled: _____

_____

_____

_____

My thoughts and feelings about the third archetype I circled: _____

_____

_____

_____

This list of archetypes here is just a sampling of the dozens of archetypes that Carl Jung and others have identified. You'll encounter even more archetypes in this book. But for now, contemplating just a few of the ones I've mentioned can move you further into understanding yourself and how you've lived your life up until this point. In addition to what you've written here, you might want to explore the other archetypes and their effect on you and your story. Note that archetypes often express themselves in roles you play in your life, a topic you'll learn more about shortly.

Identifying More Archetypes That Are Influencing You

Carl Jung identified some other archetypes that are worth thinking about. They include the shadow, the animus or anima, and the persona.

The Shadow

The shadow is a collection of the repressed parts of ourselves, both positive and negative, that we keep in the unconscious to avoid discomfort. Whatever you're ashamed of, whatever you're afraid to claim for yourself because you would feel inauthentic or unworthy of having that quality or desire, is part of your shadow.

If you can think of some aspects of yourself that you're ashamed of, consider writing about them here:

I'm ashamed of: _____

_____

_____

_____

Maybe there's some aspect of yourself you'd like to believe is there, but you feel guilty or like an imposter if you were to say, *This is a part of who I am*. This aspect of yourself could reflect a quality that's positive—after all, every quality has its plusses and minuses. You might want to write about this aspect of yourself here and why you have trouble acknowledging that part of yourself:

I'd like to think of myself as someone who: _____

_____

_____

_____

It's hard for me to acknowledge this aspect of myself because: _____

_____

_____

_____

In working with your unconscious and uncovering your shadow, you'll be able to relate differently to the parts of yourself that you've denied. You might free yourself from feelings of shame or inadequacy and discover positive qualities you hadn't acknowledged before or that you undervalued. The Everyday Person might not be so boring and irritating after all. The Adventurer might express itself very creatively, renewing your sense of vitality. The Healer might help you find a new path for yourself. The Fool might help you in unexpected ways.

You can relate differently to parts of yourself that you have denied, freeing yourself from feelings of shame and inadequacy.

The Animus and Anima

Jung believed that we all have unconscious contrasexual opposites that can give us more insights into ourselves. He said that men have an *anima*, which is Latin for *soul*, and women have an *animus*, the masculine version of *soul*. You might find yourself encountering an opposite sex figure in a dream or a visualization. If so, pay attention, because it may be telling you something about your hidden beliefs regarding masculinity and femininity, beliefs that may be causing you to remain stuck in a story that you don't like. In fact, any dream about a man or a woman might be trying to tell you something about masculinity, femininity, and your relationship to these archetypal energies.

The following journaling prompts can help you better understand your experiences and beliefs about masculinity, femininity, manhood, and womanhood.

Some qualities I associate with masculinity and being a man: _____
_____
_____
_____

When it comes to these qualities, here is what I feel and think about them and whether I have them (or want to have them): _____
_____
_____
_____

Some qualities I associate with femininity and being a woman: _____
_____
_____
_____

When it comes to these qualities, here is what I feel and think about them and whether I have them (or want to have them): _____
_____
_____
_____

Who, if anyone, represents the ideal man to me, and why: _____

_____

_____

Who, if anyone, represents the ideal woman to me, and why: _____

_____

_____

My blend of masculine and feminine qualities looks like this: _____

_____

_____

_____

The Persona

The persona is the face you show to the world. As you think about how others see you, you can answer these questions to gain insights about how you see yourself and how others see you.

How would you describe yourself? _____

_____

_____

How would people who know you well describe you? _____

_____

_____

How would people who have only briefly met you describe you? _____

_____

_____

Is there something you'd like people to know about you that you rarely (if ever) reveal about yourself, and if so, what is it? _____

_____

_____

Roles You Play

Archetypes often express themselves in the roles we play in our lives and how we inhabit them. You might want to think about your roles—in your interactions with others and in the stories you tell yourself about your experiences.

Most roles can be thought of as archetypal. For example, your story might be *I feel as if I'm always the bridesmaid, never the bride.* That could mean you feel you're affected by the Every Person archetype, seen by others as not worthy of being the center of attention. However, you might think of the Bridesmaid as an archetype that's somewhat different from the Everyday Person. You could call it the Bridesmaid or the Underappreciated One. You might decide that you feel you're being affected by the Everyday Person archetype as well as another one: The Self-sacrificing Martyr or the Less-Than One or the Never-Chosen One, perhaps.

Below, you can name a role you play that you're not comfortable with, identify which archetype or archetypes match up with that role, and note any payoffs or drawbacks you experience because you play that role.

A role I play that I'm not comfortable with, and an archetype, or archetypes, that fit with this role: _____

_____

_____

_____

The payoffs and drawbacks to this role are: _____

_____

_____

_____

By learning from your roles and their associated archetypes, you can transform habitual behaviors and attitudes, change your story, and change the roles you play within it. Imagine feeling courageous instead of scared … valued instead of taken for granted … seen instead of overlooked … There's a movie called *The Great Santini*, starring Robert Duvall, about a man who has served in the military for so long that he has no idea how to adjust to civilian life. He acts like a warrior when he's home with his wife and kids, and it harms his relationships with them. Maybe you can identify a role that isn't working for you—a self you want to relate to differently.

Who Cast You in Your Roles?

If you allow the archetypal energies that are affecting you to remain hidden from your awareness, they will fuel life stories that may feel out of your control. The goal is to work consciously with archetypal energies—the themes, plots, and characters that reside in the collective unconscious we all share as well as in your own unconscious. If you do that, you can learn from them and change the way you relate to them so they affect you differently. The hidden-wisdom techniques you find in this book give you the power to change your story and how you relate to archetypal energies that are influencing you.

Look back at the story you just wrote and any roles you played to see if you can identify who cast you in that role. Was it you? Was your role your interpretation of how you should act—for example, were you the strict father who is emotionally unexpressive because you felt that's how a father should be based on what you saw in your family and community? If you were always the lone wolf, why did you play that role? In other words, you want to become aware of who wrote the story about how your needs and happiness are secondary to someone else's—and why you adopted that story. You might not even have realized you adopted it.

My thoughts on a role or two I've played and who cast me in that role or those roles: _____

_____

_____

_____

_____

Every role you have played in your life has qualities that you might have avoided looking at too closely because they make you feel embarrassed or insecure. If you've always been a caretaker, supporting others and not receiving support yourself, maybe you've taken some pride in that—and even pushed away help that was offered to you. That truth might not sit well with you. If you're like the Great Santini, bringing warrior energy into too many situations and acting like a general whose orders must be obeyed, recognizing that role could make you feel embarrassed or ashamed—but it's also a first step toward transformation.

The next step is to begin imagining what other aspects of yourself need to be expressed—and how. That is, you can start to identify what, if any, qualities you have been stifling.

As you think about these inner selves that have qualities that embarrass you or make it hard for you to be confident, imagine that they have strengths you've overlooked that have served you. Maybe the caretaker within you, the self who regularly supports others, needs to start helping *you* more often. Maybe your warrior self needs to fight your fear of seeming vulnerable that drives your need to be aggressive and demanding with others.

Maybe you have some ideas about inner selves that need to be expressed and how adopting new roles associated with them could help you in your life. If so, you can write below about a self/ role you'd like to adopt. If you can't identify one, don't worry. You'll have other opportunities in this book to interact with your hidden wisdom to discover what you need to let go of and bring in to change your story and, consequently, the roles you play within it.

An aspect of myself or a "role" I would like to adopt and express in my everyday life is:

_____

_____

I'd like to play this role/express this aspect of myself because: _____

_____

_____

_____

_____

Identifying Your Story

You've now identified some archetypes, themes, and storylines that are affecting you. You may have had thoughts and strong feelings related to them and not realized it. This is a good point to once again sum up the story of your life in just a sentence or two, as if you were summarizing a novel, memoir, or song. If you wrote your story earlier, notice whether your thoughts about it have changed as a result of doing the work in this book so far.

In a sentence (or two or three) that summarizes my experiences to this point in my life, my story is this: _____

_____

_____

_____

_____

In the next chapter, you'll begin to access your hidden wisdom to continue to understand and identify your story and any obstacles you have to changing it for the better. I think everyone's had the experience of wanting to transform some aspect of their life only to wonder, *Why is it so hard to change?* Working with dreams is a good way to begin the process of tapping into your hidden wisdom for insights and energies that can help you with personal transformation. You can use similar techniques for working with visualizations and journeys and what you encounter in them.

Chapter 3
Hidden Wisdom in Dreams, Visualizations, and Journeys

Through your work in this book, you've now encountered some of the archetypes that affect people. There are many more you might come across—and you might have already done so. Archetypes can appear spontaneously in our dreams and minds when we are meditating, doing a visualization, or journeying. They might come in the form of symbols, figures, or patterns of action, thought, or emotion—for example, they might express themselves as plots in dreams. Your hidden wisdom can be quite creative in communicating to you. It's important to record what it tells or shows you so that you don't forget. Your hidden wisdom may have more to tell you than you think.

Why do we dream? Some say that dreams are merely a byproduct of the brain's need to consolidate our experiences and place them into long-term memory. I believe that in addition to that role, they are a way for Source and our unconscious mind to communicate with us, sharing hidden wisdom. When we're uncomfortable with a truth about ourselves and our lives, we tend to push that knowledge out of the conscious mind. Dreams and visions can be influenced by unconscious knowledge and help you recognize what your hidden wisdom knows. So, even if you recently bought some carnations at the grocery store or saw them at a friend's house, dreaming about carnations might be both a way for your brain to consolidate the memory and a way for your hidden wisdom to tell you something. Don't dismiss a symbol or figure in your dream as insignificant because you can rationalize that it appeared because you recently encountered that object or person in your daily life.

Answering the following questions can help you start to tap into your hidden wisdom, which has knowledge about your life that might not be a part of your everyday awareness.

What, if any, symbols or figures appear regularly in your dreams? Why do you think they appear? _____

_____

_____

_____

_____

_____

If there are any symbols or figures you sense might have an important message for you, what are they and what do you think their message to you might be? _____

_____

_____

_____

_____

What, if any, storylines reoccur in your dreams? (Note: The storyline might be a very brief sequence of events.) _____

_____

_____

If you've ever had a dream so vivid that it was hard to shake the belief that it wasn't real, what was the dream and what did you make of it? _____

_____

_____

_____

_____

_____

_____

If you have seen a symbol or figure in your dream, and you're curious about its meaning, maybe because it has appeared more than once in your dreams, you can draw it or write about it here:

Working with Dreams

If your dreams haven't helped you better recognize and understand unconscious influences on you, you might want to work with a dream so you can have that experience. Pay special attention to recurrent, vivid, or frightening dreams and ones that seem especially real. They may occur when your unconscious mind is trying to tell you something important. If your unconscious mind doesn't get its message through to you in a dream, it often will try again to nudge you to pay attention.

To better remember your dreams, go to bed at night intending to remember them. When you wake up, immediately record your dreams on paper or a recording device kept on your nightstand. Let the images flow out and don't stop to try to interpret the dream or dreams. Prematurely turning on the analytical parts of your mind can shut off the part of your mind that can help you recall and learn from your dreams.

To better remember your dreams, go to bed at night intending to remember them.

Also, as your head sinks into the pillow, you can tell yourself that you intend to have a dream that will help you. It's common to be in the habit of forgetting dreams upon awakening, so if you open your eyes and feel disappointment as you remember your intention and realize you didn't have a helpful dream after all, don't give up. Lie there for a moment to see if a dream comes back to you, and if it does, record it. If it doesn't, try again the next night. It might take a while to get the helpful dream you're seeking.

To interpret your dream, keep in mind that while dream symbols can be universal, they may have a special meaning for you. Often, the temptation is to reach for a dream interpretation dictionary or look up a particular symbol online to see what it means. A better strategy is to sit and hold the symbol or memory of what happened in the dream in your mind and see if any emotions, words, or images come up for you. Move beyond the most common interpretation of a dream symbol and consider what it means to you. For example, dominoes in a dream could symbolize the domino effect of one thing leading to another. However, if you always played dominoes with your grandmother, and you stopped playing after she moved away when you were a child, the dominoes in your dream could represent something that is very personal to you.

Answering the questions below may be helpful as you do more work with dreams.

If there was an unusual symbol, figure, or place in a dream that you can remember encountering, what was it and what was unusual about it? (For example, maybe

it had odd qualities, or you had a strange emotional reaction to it, such as fearing an ordinary object or feeling very comfortable with a disturbing figure.)

_____

_____

_____

_____

_____

_____

_____

Sometimes we ignore the throwaways in a dream—things we think of as unimportant. Think about what they might be associated with to see if you gain unexpected insights. Let's say that in a dream, you're running from a lion that's hunting you, and there's a grey house in the background. That may seem an insignificant detail, but maybe it was there because it has a message for you.

Also, pay attention to your emotions within a dream if you want to better understand its message. Your emotional response to events, symbols, or figures in your dream may not make sense at first, but they may well make sense when you work with your dream for a while. Unusual emotional responses within a dream can be a clue to look more closely at what the dream images mean.

You can explore a particular dream element now (for example, a figure, an object, or a place) and answer the questions below.

How did you interact with this dream element? _____

_____

_____

_____

Does this symbol, figure, or place in a dream resemble something in your real life? If so, what is it? _____

_____

_____

_____

As you start to think about the dream and what it meant, don't be too literal in your interpretation. For example, if you dream of dying or someone else's death, it's possible that it's a literal death you're dreaming of, but it's more likely to be about a symbolic death, such as the ending of a situation. If you die in a dream, it could be that your unconscious mind is telling you that a role you're playing is coming to an end or the person you have always been has to change so you can move forward into better opportunities and circumstances. A dream about the death of others could be about changes they will make, your relationship to them transforming, or a shift in some aspect of yourself. Maybe if your mother dies in your dream, it means there's a mothering side of yourself that needs to change. Some aspect of mothering may need to die so this energy can be expressed in a new way.

As you ponder the meanings of dreams and their symbols, notice which interpretations feel right to you. Your intuition is a good guide. When you have a dream you would like to work with, recall it here and draw any specific images that came to you. I suggest you not try to interpret it until you've remembered all you can.

My dream:

If you don't have a dream you would like to interpret to gain insights about your life, set a plan for remembering a dream that will be helpful for you.

Beginning to Interpret What You Experienced and Encountered

Let your intuition guide you in finding associations between aspects of your dreams and what has happened or is happening in your life. If you do this, it will be easier to interpret what the dream has to tell you. The same is true of interpreting experiences with journeys, which you'll begin doing in later in this chapter, and visualizations, which you'll encounter in Chapter 11: Create the Life You Desire. The following questions can help you with your interpretation of a symbol, figure, sequence of events in the dream, and so on.

What emotions did you experience in the dream? _____

_____

_____

In what area of your life are you experiencing those emotions or would it make sense to feel those feelings? (You might not be consciously aware of the feelings you're having in your everyday life, so thinking about when it would make sense to have a feeling can help you identify where you might be repressing your emotions.) _____

_____

_____

What themes were integrated into your dream? (For example, being persecuted, not being heard, feeling pressured to do something you're not ready to do, etc.) _____

_____

_____

_____

If there are areas in your everyday life where these themes have shown up, what are they? ____

_____

_____

_____

_____

You can write your dream interpretation here. Later, if you wish, you can return to it and see if you have new insights into its meaning.

My interpretation of my dream is: _____

_____

_____

_____

_____

_____

_____

_____

_____

_____

Remember, the themes in your dreams are universal even though you'll have a unique experience of them. You may have had a dream with these themes because your hidden wisdom, that is, your wise inner self, guided by Source, wants you to look more closely at your beliefs about your life and what you have experienced and can experience. (You'll learn more about this inner self in Chapter 4: Working with Your Wise Inner Self.)

Dream interpretation can be remarkably helpful for enacting positive changes in your life. Dreams can give you insights into situations, including insights into any obstacles you're facing in changing your story and how you might overcome them. What's more, a dream might simply have an energetic influence on you. As an analyst, I treated many patients who had breakthrough dreams. One client who suffered from a fear of leaving her home (agoraphobia) dreamed of a strange man holding her down and a neighbor coming to rescue her. She realized that in the dream, the strange man represented her late husband, who had been very controlling. For some reason she couldn't explain, after having the dream, she had a breakthrough in her ability to venture outside. The neighbor represented a positive, helpful inner energy that she had finally been able to access. I'd like to believe that the talk therapy I did with this woman and others who had breakthrough dreams set them up to experience a dramatic transformation in their feelings and responses to the situations they were in, leading them to make big changes in their lives. However, the big shifts in how they carried themselves and the boundaries they set with the people in their lives was due to their finally having a transformative dream. Over the years, I have developed deep respect for the power of dreams to support us in transformation.

Journeys and Visualizations

In this workbook, you'll encounter some journeys and visualizations that can help you access your hidden wisdom. You can think of a journey, also known as a shamanic journey, as a guided visualization where you have some specific instructions for what to imagine and some places within the journey where your imagination or intuition can speak to you without any directions from your conscious mind. You might journey to the Upper World to get insights into your future. Or you might journey to the Lower World to access a contract you didn't realize was confining you to have certain experiences and that can be renegotiated. In a guided visualization, you might visit a generic beach or forest. So, in journeying, you go to specific places that have particular qualities related to the process of transformation.

When doing a guided visualization or a journey, you are likely to encounter symbols and figures like you do in dreams. These may have important messages for you.

Also, shamans (medicine men and women who use ancient healing techniques) would say that after you leave ordinary consciousness when seated and focused on your intention to journey, you actually travel to a real place.*

There may be an advantage to looking at journeys as real experiences in realms that actually exist. Carl Jung once treated a patient who dreamed she was on the moon, and he said that he felt it was best to approach his conversation with her as if she actually had been on the moon—in other words, he accepted her reality. His approach wasn't so out there after all: We now know that the mind can experience what is imagined as if it were real. Research shows that an imagined experience can be extremely powerful for bringing about transformation. As I mentioned, I have seen clients I've treated dramatically shift their point of view and emotions after having a dream they found to be significant.

To me, it doesn't matter whether you believe a journey takes you to a real realm or you believe it's just a powerful exercise for your mind. What matters is your experience of it and how you use that experience to make changes in your life.

For now, I'd like you to try a journey.

---

* Shamans will journey on someone's behalf, bringing back insights and energy for transformation, but all the journeys in this book are ones you can do on your own. Again, if you like, you can simply think of them as powerful guided visualizations.

Guidelines for Doing the Journeys in This Book

To prepare for any journey, just as you would prepare for a guided visualization or meditation, find a time and place where you won't be disturbed. Then, set an intention to experience insights and perhaps an energy exchange (letting go of some energy and bringing in another) with the help of your wise inner self and Source. If you know you are supposed to encounter a guardian, a contract, or something else, set an intention to do that, too.

While I will give you specific instructions for each journey, it may be easier for you to recall the details if you record yourself reading them aloud. You can also use drumming, rattling, mindful breathing, or some other technique to help you get out of your analytical mind and into your intuitive one as you listen to the recording. If you like, record your own drumming or rattling as you read aloud the journey's instructions. Also, when you make the recording, be sure to leave pauses in places in the scripts where you will want to wait for your unconscious mind to give you answers or help you encounter something (for example, a contract in the Room of Contracts).

In shamanic traditions, when doing any journey, you would also open sacred space beforehand and close it afterwards, using a ritual to show Source that you respect the sacredness of the work you're doing. You would also humbly ask Source for assistance and cleanse yourself after opening sacred space. If you don't want to create such a ritual, you could simply:

- approach this work with respect and solemnity
- imagine yourself letting go of any blocks to communicating with the hidden wisdom that's available to you
- ask Source (or pray to God) to help you
- end the journey by thanking Source for Source's help and make a point of waiting for a few moments to return to ordinary consciousness
- after the journey, feel and express to Source gratitude for the experience

Also, remember that in journeys, you'll encounter a guardian, which represents your wise inner self that wants to protect you from facing anything too stressful for you. You don't necessarily have to *see* this guardian in your mind's eye—or see anything else that is suggested in a journey script. It's enough to know it's there and work with it as the script instructs you to.

Hidden-Wisdom Technique: Journey to the Room of Contracts to Change a Hidden Belief

This hidden-wisdom technique is heavily influenced by one I learned when studying and later teaching shamanism at The Four Winds Society. Its founder, Alberto Villoldo, taught what he had learned from healers in the Andes mountains in South America, who wanted people to share their wisdom teachings and practices. Over the years, I went from student to teacher and created my own versions of some of his exercises.

The first journey you will take is to the Room of Contracts. You can prepare for it by setting an intention to uncover a hidden contract that has been shaping your unconscious beliefs so that you can destroy it and replace it with a better contract. This contract, a hidden belief about how you should live your life, which has been influencing you whether you realize it or not, has two parts: A declaration about what you should do and a declaration about what you'll experience as a result. Your contract might show up as a scroll or an inner knowing or something else, like a legal document. The contract might be something like:

- I don't speak up on my own behalf if it might upset others. That way, people will accept me and treat me well.

- I live cautiously, making safe choices so I won't get hurt.

- I will never show vulnerability so that people won't think less of me.

- If I repress my anger instead of expressing it, I will have better relationships.

- If pursue my dream of living a simpler life, I will become undisciplined and unproductive and will experience so much financial hardship that I'll become dependent on other people and not live up to my obligation to take care of myself.

Contracts like these can hold you back from living a more satisfying life. You can destroy a contract and write a new one, or you can revise the contract to serve you better—whatever feels right to you. The new contract should make a statement about how you'll act in the future. The statement should be followed by a statement about the payoff to acting in this new way. Because there will be some payoffs to retaining some aspect of the contract, you'll want to ask your wise inner self how you could write a new contract that would have payoffs as good as or even better than the old contract had. Your wise inner self might offer you invaluable insights into how to achieve the payoffs, or even better ones, by agreeing to a new contract.

What will your new contract be? Perhaps something like:

- I will speak my truth even if it hurts people, not hurting them unnecessarily but not stifling my voice either. Then, I'll be true to myself, develop confidence, and yet also have others respect my opinions and wishes.

- When faced with the opportunity to take a risk, I will tune into my wise inner self for guidance rather than always playing it safe. That way, I will know which risks to take and which to avoid. Consequently, I'll have fewer regrets about the choices I've made.

- I will learn from my wise inner self how and when to let myself be vulnerable. This way, I won't be closed off from emotional intimacy with others and won't set myself up to be hurt unnecessarily.

- If I express my anger in healthy ways, I will have better relationships.

- If I pursue my dream of living a simpler life, I will be disciplined and productive and make enough money to be independent and take care of myself.

A new contract will help you to have a more satisfying story and a life that is in synch with your values and priorities. Additionally, you can always come back to discover more contracts that are worth changing and alter them in any way you like.

To begin the journey, be sure to free yourself of distractions, take a seat, settle in comfortably, close your eyes, and focus on your breathing to help you attain a meditative state. Ask Spirit and any spirit helpers you have to assist you in this important work of discovering and rewriting the contracts that have been stifling you, preventing you from living a more fulfilling life that aligns with your deepest held beliefs and desires.

When you are ready, begin.

Script for the Journey to the Room of Contracts to Change a Hidden Belief

Imagine yourself descending a spiral staircase that takes you deep into the earth, knowing that by going beneath the surface of your conscious awareness, you can do work that is harder to do when you are in an ordinary mind-state.

Keep walking down the stairs. Let go of your everyday concerns. Brush aside any distractions as you continue to descend. Continue climbing downward until you reach the bottom of the staircase, where you'll feel solid ground beneath your feet.

Look to your side and notice your wise inner self is there to accompany you on this journey and protect you from going further if it might be difficult for you to handle this work today. Ask your wise inner self, *Is today a good day for me to journey?* Wait for the answer.

If the answer is no, ask your wise inner self if there's something you must do to be granted permission to continue your work down here below your conscious awareness. For example, is there something you must acknowledge? Something you must let go of? Something you must promise yourself and your wise inner self?

Listen to what this self has to say, and make your choice, either returning up the spiral staircase with the intention to try the journey again some other day or doing as your wise inner self says so you can continue the journey. You can negotiate if you don't want to do as your wise inner self says, but it's best to follow its advice. After all, your wise inner self is looking out for your best interests.

Now that you have permission, begin walking, with your wise inner self at your side, toward a building ahead of you …

As you approach it, observe that this one-room building is a place where contracts are stored. When you reach the building's entrance, stand before its door and ask, *Show me a contract I can encounter that will give me insight into my story and beliefs about what I can and should experience.* Wait a moment …

Now open the door. Observe what is behind it: a contract you made unconsciously. The contract may show itself to you as a scroll that unfurls before your eyes or something else. It may be a contract that you hear in your mind's ear. Read, listen to, or intuit what the contract says about the payoff you will receive for making certain choices and maintaining certain habits …

What does it say?

Now turn to your wise inner self and let this self know that you are going to destroy this contract to write a new, better one. Ask if there is anything you should know before taking your intended action …

Take the old contract, in whatever form it appears, and destroy it or transform it. Notice the tools for writing a new contract or revising the old one appear before you. Use them to write a new, better contract …

Turn to your wise inner self and ask, *Have I left anything out of this contract?* Listen for the answer and revise the contract if you like …

Now ask your wise inner self, *Is there anything else I need to learn or do before leaving this room of contracts?* Consider the counsel of your wise inner self. You do not have to take this advice if you don't want to. When working with your wise inner self, you are always in charge.

When you're ready, leave the contract in the room and depart, with your wise inner self at your side. Close the door, turn your back on the building that houses the room of contracts, and walk back to the place at the bottom of the spiral staircase you descended earlier …

When you are ready to climb the staircase back to ordinary consciousness, thank your wise inner self for helping, and then ascend the stairs, climbing upward until you feel your journey is done and you are ready to open your eyes.

Thank Spirit and any spirit helpers (a guardian angel, spirit guides such as power or spirit animals, etc.) for their assistance on the journey you just took. Then, you can write about your experiences and your impressions, including what the old contract said and what the new one says.

What your old contract was: _____

_____

_____

_____

What your new contract is: _____

_____

_____

_____

Any other notes on/observations regarding your experience in the room of contracts: _____

_____

_____

_____

_____

_____

_____

_____

If you'd like to draw something you saw or experienced in the room of contracts, do so here:

If You Get No Response from Your Unconscious

Once when I was journeying, I encountered my wise inner self, whom I call Wise Inner Carl. *Why do I have to experience so many problems and upsetting situations in my life?* I asked Wise Inner Carl. He only smiled, and I realized that was all I was going to get out of him for now! I realized that I needed to figure out the answers for myself at this point—but considered returning to Wise Inner Carl for another dialogue later to learn more. (In Chapter 4: Working with Your Wise Inner Self, I'll teach you how to dialogue.)

When you get no response from an aspect of your unconscious that you're trying to work with—when no images, sensations, ideas, or words come to you—go ahead and ask more questions or repeat the question you asked. Be patient, knowing you might not get answers at first. You might need to do another journey, or a dialogue, at another time. I chose to dialogue with Wise Inner Carl after the journey in which I met him, and I asked why he couldn't answer my question about my experiencing a lot of turbulence. His answer was, *You need to go through difficulties and draw your own conclusions about their meaning. When you start doing this more often, you'll realize that you have a lot of expectations about what you should experience that keep you stuck in conflicts. Be more open-minded and accepting of life and of other people, and you won't feel so burdened by problems and conflicts.*

In journeying or doing a guided visualization, you might gain a simple insight: *learn to laugh,* for example, or *give yourself time.* You might simply feel lighthearted or re-experience a memory of laughing. You might see a clock with a second hand that slows down. Remember, the message might not come to you as words but as another symbol, or a feeling or sensation. Later, you can sit with the message until you understand it. Again, don't let your logical mind interfere with this process—don't try to figure out what a symbol means or why a certain figure came to you. Let your intuition suggest the answers to your questions. An image might mean something different for you than what you initially believe.

Keep in mind that it's common to have difficulty opening up to a message from your unconscious because it can make you feel embarrassed or ashamed. When you accept that you might encounter a difficult truth, when you're willing to let go of beliefs and feelings that are blocking you from experiencing what you would like to experience, change becomes much easier. The author Denis Waitley once said, "It's not who you are that holds you back, it's who you think you are not." When you access your hidden wisdom, you can discover obstacles to becoming the person you want to be—and gain insights and energy for overcoming them.

So, even if you're dissatisfied with the answers you receive through journeying, doing guided visualizations, or dialoguing, even if you're frustrated at the lack of answers and clarity, keep doing the work. With practice, it will become easier to access wisdom from your unconscious.

In the next chapter, you'll learn more about working with your wise inner self. This self has much hidden wisdom for you and will help you identify your story—the real one, which you might not have acknowledged. It will also enable you to discover ways in which your story is influencing your life. You can consciously choose to access this wise inner self by learning to change your brainwaves and state of consciousness naturally, using your mind and some simple techniques.

Chapter 4
Working with Your Wise Inner Self

You met your wise inner self on your Journey to the Room of Contracts to Change a Hidden Belief. Now it's time to become better acquainted with this inner figure.

The wise inner self is the aspect of yourself that knows your deepest yearnings and your story—the one you're living according to, not necessarily the one you tell yourself and others. Guided by Spirit, your wise inner self can help you consciously craft a new story, assisting you as you reframe your past and present and develop a more optimistic view of your future.

The Wise Inner Self and the Archetypes

Your wise inner self will help you as you work with the collective unconscious, our shared pool of memories, stories, and archetypal characters. The archetypal stories we live according to are very powerful, programming our thoughts, feelings, and actions—even our health. From the collective unconscious, we can bring in new stories that give us the momentum to change our lives. We can access new energies that can help us step into different roles or inhabit our familiar roles differently. In short, because of your access to the collective unconscious, you have many resources for transformation to draw upon. Your wise inner self can help you discover them.

We can bring in new energies that can help us step into different roles or inhabit our familiar roles differently.

What Your Wise Inner Self Can Express to You

Often, people who use techniques for accessing the unconscious mind come to realize that the insights they've gained were ones the conscious mind may not have been aware of, yet they weren't completely unaware of them. It's easy to become distracted by all the voices outside of us that tell us what we should think, believe, and feel and what we should do—and to ignore that small voice within that is our intuition or wise inner self speaking to us.

We might become uneasy with the truth because it intimidates us. Returning to Carl Jung's idea of shadow qualities within that we don't want to look at, you might think that we're only uncomfortable discovering seemingly negative qualities such as being cruel, selfish, or overly competitive. But you might also be embarrassed by qualities such as gentleness, vulnerability, or playfulness. These archetypal energies are often hidden from our conscious mind, and we might only connect with them through dreams or intuition. Or because we're denying them, they might play out in our lives in ways that we don't like. Instead of letting ourselves be gentle, for example, we might suppress that quality and overreact when someone else is gentle, ridiculing them with a sarcastic remark.

When our inner truth contradicts the voices of influential people outside of us, such as the people we love, we might repress it, but it remains in our unconscious, where it can be accessed. The unconscious mind nudges us by bringing us messages in dreams and symbols that may come to us when we choose to stop thinking about how to solve our problems and instead sit quietly in a state of openness.

Trust that you know more than you think you know and be willing to listen to your wise inner self. I found it very satisfying to guide a client into claiming for herself what she already knew deep down and to help her see that I was merely an assistant in her healing process.

Where do these insights we find within ourselves originate? Maybe Spirit, working with us, plants the seeds, tends to the sprouts, and offers us a harvest of wisdom that is hidden within. Maybe our individual unconscious is, as Carl Jung suggested, always connected to a collective unconscious that's filled with wisdom and insights as well as archetypal energies that can affect us in good ways and in not-so-good ways. We can work with these energies to create better outcomes for ourselves and heal what's causing us to suffer.

Whatever you believe about the origin and nature of your hidden wisdom, you can learn to listen to it more often and explore what you can learn. You might want to think about a time when you realized that you intuitively knew or felt something and write about it here.

Something I intuited: _____

_____

_____

_____

_____

_____

If I dismissed my intuition, here's what happened (and what the results were): _____

_____

_____

If I listened to my intuition, here's what happened (and what the results were): _____

_____

_____

Looking back at these experiences, and perhaps some others involving my intuition, here's what I think about my intuition: _____

_____

_____

Intuition is a gift we all have, but we might not remember that we possess it. There are many gifts we might overlook. The following journey, to the Room of Treasures to Gain Insights and Energy for Change, will help you to discover some that could help you in your quest for transformation. Remember to prepare for it and work with it as you learned earlier, and afterward, don't forget to express gratitude to Spirit and any spirit helpers for what you discover.

Hidden-Wisdom Technique: Journey to the Room of Treasures to Gain Insights and Energy for Change

Now that you've altered a contract that has been influencing your story, using the Journey to the Room of Contracts to Change a Hidden Belief, you've freed yourself from the burden of expectations you didn't know you had. By destroying the contract, you liberated energy for living your life differently, according to a story consciously written by you, one that is in greater alignment with what you truly desire. However, keep in mind that all of us have many contracts or hidden beliefs. There may be more contracts you wish to destroy and replace, but for now, you're going to access a treasure that has energy you can bring into your body and its energy field that surrounds it. This new energy is a treasure that can help you live according to your new contract and achieve the transformation you seek. For example, you could receive a spear that will help you get to the point or a spinning top to remind you to stay balanced even when you're busy.

The energy will appear in the form of a symbol, a sound, words, music, a thought, or something else. You can use your imagination or your hands to sweep it into your body as you sit in a meditative state during this journey. In this way, you are giving yourself fuel for transformation. (Like the Journey to the Room of Contracts to Change a Hidden Belief, the Journey to the Room of Treasures to Gain Insights and Energy for Change was influenced by a journey I learned when being trained in shamanic practice at The Four Winds Society.)

To journey to the Room of Treasures, begin as you did with the journey to the Room of Contracts: Remove all distractions, sit comfortably with closed eyes, and ask for Spirit and any spirit helpers to assist you as you take this journey. Focus on your breathing, refocusing whenever necessary, so that you bring yourself into a meditative state that differs from ordinary consciousness. Set your intention, start your recording if you're using one, and prepare to discover a treasure whose energy will benefit you.

Script for the Journey to the Room of Treasures to Gain Insights and Energy for Change

Imagine there is a spiral staircase into the earth, going deep beneath the surface of your ordinary awareness. Begin to descend the stairs. Continue until you reach the lower world where the Room of Treasures resides …

Notice your wise inner self standing there, waiting for you. Ask whether today is a good day for you to journey. If the answer is no, ask whether there is something you can do to gain permission to continue journeying today. Listen to what this self has to say, and make your choice, either returning up the spiral staircase with the intention to try the journey again some other day or doing as your wise inner self says, so you can continue the journey. You can negotiate if you don't want to do as your wise inner self says, but it's best to follow this advice. After all, your wise inner self is looking out for your best interests.

If you are going to end your journey, or do something to gain permission, do so now …

If you are going to continue, begin to walk forward toward a building in the distance, your wise inner self at your side. This building houses the Room of Treasures, and as you approach it, you'll see it has a door. Stop before it, open the door, and ask, *What treasure do you have for me today that can help me change my story in positive ways?* Enter the room and look around until you know what treasure you are claiming … Be open to whatever form it takes.

Remain present with your treasure and its meaning for you … Then, use your imagination or your hands to sweep it into your body. Place the energy wherever you sense you need it. This energy will be there for you whenever you want to draw on it to maintain your commitment to living differently …

When you are ready, with your wise inner self at your side, close the door to the Room of Treasures and head back to the spiral staircase you climbed down earlier. Feel the new energy in your body and energy field …

When you reach the base of the staircase, thank your wise inner self for this assistance … Now, ascend the stairs until you are ready to return to ordinary consciousness …

When you are ready, open your eyes and thank Spirit and any spirit helpers for being your allies on this journey. Then, you can write about what you experienced.

Notes on my journey to the Room of Treasures: _____

_____

_____

_____

_____

_____

_____

_____

_____

If you would like to draw something you saw or experienced in the Room of Treasures, do so here:

Hidden-Wisdom Technique: Dialoguing

To learn more from whatever you encounter in a dream, guided visualization, or journey, you can also do a dialogue. Dialoguing is an invaluable tool for communicating with what is in your unconscious. The conversation can be between you and a figure or symbol you encounter in a dream, guided visualization, or journey—or something that you simply know you want to learn from, such as:

- your resistance to change

- an emotion

- a mindset (frustration, disappointment, pessimism, etc.)

- an archetypal energy or theme (betrayal, compassion, responsibility, etc.)

- an aspect of yourself (your wise inner self, your adventurous self, your scared self, etc.)

The dialoguing process I created is drawn from Gestalt therapy (*gestalt* means "many parts connected") as well as Jungian active imagination. The idea is to encounter insights and energies for transformation that will shake you up to some degree, so you don't remain in the same old state of wishing to but not changing the way you say you'd like to change. When interpreting dreams or experiences you had when accessing your hidden wisdom, it's easy to let your biases and analytical mind guide you. Dialoguing helps you to face truths you might otherwise keep buried in your unconscious.

To dialogue, find a quiet place where you won't be disturbed and can sit with your eyes closed, focusing on your breathing or a mantra, a word you repeat to focus on one thing and not become distracted. Set an intention to gain insights, and even to let go of unneeded energies and bring in energies that can help you in your pursuit of transformation or a particular goal.

Next, choose what you want to dialogue with, letting your intuition guide you. If you decide to dialogue with a figure, don't choose one that is a living person as you don't want to somehow affect them without their permission. So, if you dreamed of being angry at an old friend, you might dialogue with the anger you felt when you interacted with him in your dream.

In your dialogue, you're going to ask at least three questions. They are:

- *What insights do you have for me?*
- *What do I need to let go of?*
- *What do I need to bring in?*

If you agree to let go of or release something, you might want to sweep your hands outward or inward to see if that makes you feel as if you exchanged an old energy for a new one. You can also use this sweeping motion to energetically absorb something that you learn will benefit you.

When you're ready to start your dialogue, you can ask God or Spirit and any spiritual allies you might have (a guardian angel, spirit guides, power animals—also known as spirit animals, and so on) to offer you protection and guidance as you consult with your unconscious. You can also ask the loving universe, the saints, your wise inner self, or God or Spirit to help you. Use whatever words feel right for you in asking for this help, drawing upon your own spiritual beliefs.

Earlier, you learned techniques for taking yourself out of ordinary consciousness. You can use them now and even ritually cleanse your energy field by waving a feather to brush away unwanted energies. You can also just cleanse yourself using your imagination. In this way, you'll be ridding yourself of any energy that will make dialoguing difficult for you.

Next, focus on your breathing or a mantra, drawing your attention back to it again and again whenever it wanders. Don't worry about how often your mind seems to jump around or run with some train of thought. With practice, you'll find you are redirecting your mind less often as you begin your meditation.

When you are relaxed, begin the dialogue.

Ask your dialoguing partner, *What insights can you give me?*

Next, you're going to imagine yourself embodying whatever you are dialoguing with. It might be easier to do this if you work with a chair that is facing you, placed a few feet away from where you're sitting. Once you've asked your dialoguing partner for insights, you can walk over to the chair, sit down, and imagine you have become your dialoguing partner. Then, answer your question as this dialoguing partner. If you find this difficult to do, you might want to work with a stone placed on the chair. When you go to sit in the chair to embody your dialoguing partner, pick up the stone and blow into it the energy of this dialoguing partner. Then, take a seat, holding the rock, imagining it is transferring the energy of your dialoguing partner into you. This might make it easier to answer the questions you've posed.

With any dialogue, there are three selves present: your questioning self, the self that is the dialoguing partner you are embodying to answer, and your conscious, observing self, which is watching the process unfold. Your observing self may notice that you're being defensive or you're resistant to embodying your dialoguing partner because you want to control its answer.

Whether or not you use an extra chair and/or a rock to help you dialogue, make sure that before answering the questions you pose, you imagine yourself as embodying your dialoguing partner. You want to be sure you answer as that self, not as your questioning or observing self. Otherwise, your analytical mind may provide an answer that isn't coming from your unconscious. You're looking to learn from your hidden wisdom, not your logical mind.

When embodying your dialoguing partner, wait for the answer to your questioning self's query to arise naturally. It might come as an inner knowing, an image, or a word or words. Again, don't analyze the message. Simply note it. Then, convey the answer to the self that asked the question.

Next, arise from the chair and, if you've been working with a rock, place it back on the seat before walking over to the chair you were sitting on when you posed your question. This change in positioning can be helpful in the dialoguing process.

Each time you have received an answer from your dialoguing partner, you'll find you have ideas for more questions, just as you would if you were dialoguing with another person. You might ask for clarification or ask, *what can I give you?* or *what can you give me?* These might elicit different answers from: *what do I need to release?* and *what do I need to bring in?* You can also ask questions such as:

What can you tell me about the dream I had?

What can you tell me about yourself?

Why did you appear to me when I was on a journey?

By asking questions about what to release, you might receive not only an insight but a sense or feeling that you're letting go of something that has been weighing you down or holding you back. This release of the old energy opens space for something new to come in, which can happen with the answer to, *what do I need to bring in?* Psychologically, it makes sense that if we let go of something, such as an old way of thinking, we clear the way for something different to replace it. And if you ask for what you can bring in, you might feel an energetic shift, as if you're taking in the energy of what it is you'd like to receive: forgiveness, hope, courage, or something else.

When you're finished with your dialogue, return to your original seat and thank your dialoguing partner for this help. If you believe loving spiritual entities helped you gain insights and energies for transformation, honor them by offering them your gratitude. In fact, in asking, *is there anything I can give you or do for you*, you're honoring what you're dialoguing with. That's important because ultimately, your wise inner self—that is, your unconscious, which contains hidden wisdom—is guided by Source, who loves you and wants to help you. Respect for the help you receive keeps your ego in check and helps you stay open to insights and energies you might otherwise resist because you think they won't benefit you.

Asking questions in a dialogue can yield clarification and insights as well as an energetic exchange. The energetic shift you experience in a dialogue can be quite powerful for bringing about transformation.

The dialoguing process might seem confusing at first, but it will become clearer with practice. Plus, you'll be amazed at what your conscious self can learn from your unconscious parts, your dialoguing partners. Unlike advice from someone else, the guidance you receive in this process is from deep within you—from your own hidden wisdom.

Here's what a dialogue might look like.

QUESTIONER: Hello, broken bicycle that appeared to me when I set an intention to dream about my relationship with my mother. What insights do you have for me?

(The broken bicycle shows itself as an image to the questioner, who gets the sense that she has the tools to fix it but doesn't know what they are or how to use them.)

QUESTIONER: Can you tell me more?

BROKEN BICYCLE: Start fixing the relationship. You need two wheels working for the relationship to work. They work together, and you're not working together with your mother collaboratively.

QUESTIONER: Well, what can I let go of to fix the relationship?

BROKEN BICYCLE: Your need to be right.

QUESTIONER: I don't like hearing that, but I'm listening. I can be very stubborn. Is there anything else I need to release?

BROKEN BICYCLE: Mom.

(The questioner sits with the word after she hears it in her head. Then, she asks another question based on her intuitive understanding.)

QUESTIONER: Did you tell me to let go of Mom because you want me to let go of my focus on her being my mother and relate to her differently?

BROKEN BICYCLE: Yes! She is your mom but she's also a person who has her own needs and desires, her own challenges and habits.

QUESTIONER: Thank you. Remembering that might help me be more open-minded about her feelings and less self-centered.

(She pushes away the energy of needing to be right and the energy of seeing her mother only as her mother.)

QUESTIONER: OK, so, what can I bring in to fix my relationship with my mom?

BROKEN BICYCLE: Patience. You will need it to be a better listener. You want to know all the tools to use, how to use them, and how to fix everything right now. You talk over your mother, interrupting her and speaking intensely, to convince her to change in the ways you think she should change. Patience will help you slow down and listen. Leave pauses when she's talking before you start to talk. Give her breathing room to express herself.

QUESTIONER: I can see that. I'm going to bring patience into myself. (She reaches out her hands and begins sweeping into her body and energy field the energy of patience.)

QUESTIONER: Thank you for helping me. I may end up doing that. I tend to look for a quick fix or a simple answer, but I need to be patient as I work on this relationship.

If you do a dialogue, you can write about it here.

I dialogued with: _____
_____
_____
_____

My dialogue went like this: _____
_____
_____
_____
_____
_____
_____
_____
_____
_____
_____
_____
_____
_____
_____
_____
_____
_____
_____
_____
_____

After doing a dialogue, it's a good idea to write about your experiences and impressions and let yourself ponder them. If you still have questions, you can do another dialogue—with the same dialoguing partner or another one. For example, the questioner whose dialogue you read earlier might decide to dialogue again with the broken bicycle or dialogue with her frustration with her relationship with her mother, her wise inner self, or something else. You might learn something unexpected if you dialogue about a topic with different partners.

Three Crucial Questions and an Energy Exchange

When using hidden-wisdom techniques of journeying and dialoguing to engage various energies, it's often helpful to use these three key questions to your hidden wisdom, as these set the foundation for an energy exchange:

- *What insights do you have for me?*

- *What do I need to let go of?*

- *What do I need to bring in?*

Your hidden wisdom might tell you to let go of an unemotional, excessively analytical energy, which is causing you to overthink a problem, and bring in a playful one that will help you to become curious and open to new ideas and opportunities. You might need to let go of an energy of fear that you didn't even recognize was affecting you and bring in an energy of courage. After letting go of one energy, you make space for another to take its place. For example, you might need to bring in an energy of adventurousness.

Acknowledging the need to let go of one energy and bring in another seems to make it easier to experience an internal shift that supports you in making changes. Remember, when asking the questions, you might want to use your hands to draw in or push away energy as you become aware of what to let go of and what to bring in. You'll also find a ritual for releasing and bringing in energies in Chapter 12: Resilience When Presented with Life's Suddenlies that can help you feel this exchange.

When using hidden-wisdom techniques of journeying and dialoguing to engage various energies, it's often helpful to use these three key questions to your hidden wisdom, as these set the foundation for an energy exchange:

- *What insights do you have for me?*

- *What do I need to let go of?*

- *What do I need to bring in?*

By working with your hidden wisdom and doing an energy exchange, you set yourself up to more easily make changes you desire.

You've now learned more about your wise inner self and how to work with it. You've come to understand how it relates to archetypal energies and other potential dialoguing partners and discovered how it can help you improve your relationships. Now it's time to look again at your story and make a genuine commitment to change—or not. You might want to simply make some changes around the margins rather than change your story significantly. If you do that, you're less likely to unconsciously resist the transformation you think you want to experience. Being honest with yourself is the first step in changing your story for the better, so you'll be working again with your wise inner self to be sure that you're ready to make changes. And if you find you're not ready, you'll discover any obstacles that are standing in your way. With the help of your wise inner self and rituals that speak to your unconscious desire to rise above your fears, you can begin to break through any barriers to making changes you long to make.

Chapter 5
Your Story and How You Can Change It

In Chapter 2: Meet the Archetypal Energies You'll Engage, you identified your story and themes and archetypes that seem to have affected you—or that may still be influencing you. Look at that story and ask yourself, are you truly satisfied with it? And if not, what about it would you like to change? What would you like your new story to look like?*

If you had difficulty identifying your story, you might be ready to do so now.

My story is: _____

_____

_____

_____

When I look at my story up to this point, here is how I feel about it and an idea about what I would like to change it to: _____

_____

_____

_____

_____

_____

_____

_____

_____

_____

_____

---

* If you would like to work further with your story, you might want to look at my book *Change Your Story, Change Your Life: Using Jungian and Shamanic Tools for Personal Transformation.*

Stories That Aren't Working for You

Our attitudes toward our stories are often reflected in what we say to others when they say, *How are you doing?* Many of us respond, *Fine* or *Okay*, and add, *How are you doing?* Even if we're not doing okay, we may not like to admit to ourselves and others our true stories, which may be ones that make us feel sad or discouraged.

When others ask us questions about our lives, our answers may be stories that reflect our stuckness and perceived helplessness. You might tell a story like, *Everyone in my family has bad luck, so I haven't tried to find a new job even though I can't stand the one I have.* Or you might say, *No, I haven't tried meditation. I know they say it can help with anxiety, but anxiety runs in my family. I've always been an anxious person and probably always will be.*

Maybe you take a certain comfort in a story called, *This is how my life always has been. There's no point in pretending it could ever be otherwise* or *This is just who I am. I can't change*, because the story is familiar and doesn't inspire you to take risks. Stepping out of an old story could lead to failure, hurt, and disappointment, but it could also lead to a more satisfying life.

Maybe you feel your old story works well enough—but are you sure you don't want something better? You might want to consider the payoffs to sticking with your familiar story and not taking the risk of changing it versus the payoffs of transformation.

Payoffs to my familiar story that I might lose if I were to change it: _____

_____

_____

_____

_____

Things I'm not experiencing now that I might experience as payoffs to changing my familiar story and living according to a new one: _____

_____

_____

_____

_____

_____

_____

Allow yourself to imagine ways to get the payoffs you have enjoyed, or better ones, even though you change your story.

It can be distressing and demoralizing to try to improve your life only to fail or be frustrated by slow progress and setbacks. Giving up hope can seem like a sensible choice that can spare you further emotional pain. But what if you could tolerate that discomfort? You might be overestimating how hard it is to change and underestimating the enthusiasm, excitement, and joy you would feel if you were to free yourself from the familiar. Even if you've failed again and again to overcome your challenges and make big changes you say you want to make, working at changing your story can help you feel more vitalized and energetic.

A new story that includes an idea like *I appreciate what's good in my life, prioritizing the nourishment of my soul and opening myself up to new possibilities* can help you find the courage to take risks and imagine better circumstances and how you can start to bring them about.

Your new story doesn't have to be *I've solved my problems once and for all and never have to think about them again.* That isn't realistic. But imagine if you rewrote a story about having bad luck, replacing it with a new one that contains an idea like *I'm exploring and looking at my options so I can start envisioning myself in a job I find rewarding*? Or you might adopt a new story that includes an idea like *I'm going to meditate more often because I am feeling it's helping me with my anxiety.*

What Will Your New Story Be?

If you're not sure what you would like to change, consider the following chapters in your life story and whether you would like to make changes in them.

Changes I'd like to make/experience regarding my health: _____

_____

_____

_____

_____

Changes I'd like to make/experience regarding my relationships: _____

_____

_____

_____

_____

Changes I'd like to make/experience regarding my psychology (thoughts, feelings, mindsets, worldviews): _____

_____

_____

_____

_____

Changes I'd like to make/experience regarding my job, career, or vocation: _____

_____

_____

_____

_____

Changes I'd like to make/experience regarding my relationship with God/Spirit/my Higher Power: _____

_____

_____

_____

_____

Changes I'd like to make/experience regarding being of service in the world: _____

_____

_____

_____

_____

Changes I'd like to make/experience regarding money and wealth: _____

_____

_____

_____

_____

Changes I'd like to make/experience regarding time and time management: _____

_____

_____

_____

_____

Changes I'd like to make/experience regarding sexuality: _____
_____
_____
_____
_____

Wishing to change isn't enough. You need actionable, achievable goals. Even if you start by making only little changes, they can lead to big ones. Look back at the list of changes you would like to make and pick one or two that are most important to you. Set a small, specific goal for each of the one or two changes you know you would like to make. You might also set a goal for working with this book. Perhaps you'll decide that every Wednesday and Sunday night, you'll work with this workbook for at least twenty minutes.

As with all the other places in this book where you're prompted to set goals, you'll want to hold yourself accountable for achieving them. You'll also want to discover what if any obstacles stand in your way—and what works for you when it comes to goal achievement. Note that from here to the end of the book, whenever you see a target icon, it's a place where you can record a specific goal and come back later to report on whether you met it. You'll also see a checkmark icon to indicate where you can write about what did and didn't work in achieving your goal. I suggest that each time you set a specific goal, you open your calendar to the date by which you want to have met the goal and make note of your deadline there along with the page number where you wrote the goal in this workbook. This way, you can easily come back to the book and reflect on your success (or failure).

Keeping in mind the need for accountability, I'm setting this specific, achievable goal for contemplation and self-discovery: _____
_____
_____

I achieved my goal: Yes No (Circle one)

Any notes on what helped or hindered me in trying to reach my goal: _____
_____
_____

Remember, whenever you encounter the target icon in this book, you'll have a chance to set a specific goal that includes a time frame for achieving it, so you'll hold yourself accountable.

You might not have control over when you can try to meet the goal. For example, let's say you set a goal regarding what you'll do if you find yourself in a conflict with someone. In that case, you could remind yourself of the goal each morning and aim to meet it when a conflict arises. If you set a goal to be more emotionally expressive with your family, you could set an intention to do it at some point in the day every day for a week or two, checking in at the end of each day to see if you achieved your goal.

If you're struggling to come up with a goal, here are some ideas related to the life story chapters suggested earlier:

- *Health*: With the goal of losing weight, I'll reduce my consumption of sugary beverages to once a week and check in with myself at the end of every week for the next month.

- *Relationships*: With the goal of reinforcing my sense of connection to people I care about, I will compliment, thank, or hug one of these individuals at least once a day every day for the next week.

- *Psychology*: With the goal of feeling more grateful and positive, every night for three weeks before going to bed, I will write down three things for which I feel gratitude.

- *Job, career, or vocation*: With the goal of having a more enjoyable job, I will spend two hours a week for the next two weeks researching ways to make my job more exciting or pleasant. Alternatively, you could research other jobs and reflect on whether you want to stick with the one you have and try to make it more enjoyable and/or lucrative.

- *Relationship to Spirit*: With the goal of strengthening my sense of connection to Spirit, I will pray and meditate for at least five minutes three mornings a week right after waking up, for three weeks in a row.

- *Service*: With the goal of being in greater service to others, by the end of this week I will identify a volunteer opportunity in my community and set a plan for volunteering.

- *Money and wealth*: With the goal of investing more money into savings for the future, I will identify the top two or three categories where I spend the most and design a plan to reduce my monthly expenditures. I will complete my plan by the end of this month so that I can set some goals and begin implementing my plan.

- *Time management*: With the goal of opening more time for a pleasurable hobby, I will record how much time I spend watching television or using social media for one week. I will use this information to set a specific, achievable goal for reducing screentime.
- *Sexuality*: With the goal of improving my sex life, I will identify one or two issues within it and come up with one goal by the end of the week for addressing these issues over the next three months. (For example, you might express physical desire to your partner daily or carve out one date night a week.)

Persist at achieving the goal or goals you just set even if you miss the mark a few times here and there. If you find you have forgotten to do what you promised yourself you would do to stay on track to your goal, take some time to figure out what happened. Don't be hard on yourself or let disappointment in yourself stop you. In Chapter 9: If You're Not Meeting Your Goals, you'll learn about how to get unstuck if you're stalled out on the way to your goals. You'll also learn strategies for making new habits stick.

Give Yourself Credit and Have Some Faith

Your story almost surely has some aspects that are working for you. By focusing on these, you might find it easier to feel optimistic about building on them to make your life even better. You can also look at why those things are working for you and apply what you've learned to another area of your life that isn't working so well.

I suggest you write down at least five things that are working about your life. These can be from any chapter or area of your life. If you have difficulty identifying five things that are working, do the best you can to identify at least one. Then, you can write about what you are doing that contributes to these areas of your life working well for you.

Five things that are working about my life and what I'm doing to contribute to how well they're working:

1)

2)

3)

4)

5)

The next questions can help you have faith in future successes.

Are there areas in your life that are growing and thriving despite your having suffered or been hurt in some way, and if so, what are they and why do you think they're growing or thriving?

_____

_____

_____

_____

Can you identify anyone who can help you achieve success at reaching your goals, and if so, who are those helpers? _____

_____

_____

_____

_____

By now, having identified some areas of your life that aren't working, you have set at least one goal and worked toward achieving it. I want to guide you in going deeper into understanding what is and isn't working in your story and what is and isn't stopping you from changing it to be a more satisfying one. To use the hidden-wisdom techniques that follow, you'll have to be open to communicating with your wise inner self, which will be honest with you about your contributions to what is and isn't working. While we tend to blame others or external events for what's not working, the wise inner self knows whether there is something we are doing that we could change to achieve better results.

Hidden-Wisdom Technique: Depict Your Story with a Changeable Nature Painting

Your wise inner self can communicate to you through your intuition, so with this exercise, you'll be going outdoors and creating an arrangement of natural objects you find, a painting that depicts either your life story or a chapter of your story (such as your health story, relationships story, etc.).

Meditate for a few minutes to take yourself out of ordinary consciousness. You might want to ask Spirit and any other spiritual helpers to assist you and your wise inner self in creating a changeable nature painting that will give you insights into your story.

Next, find a spot to arrange objects, one that is at least several feet by several feet. You might draw a circle in the dirt or sand to contain your painting, or you might simply demarcate it in your imagination, (for example, if you're creating this painting on a patch of grass).

Gather some objects that you can use in your painting. Do this slowly, allowing your intuition to guide you into choosing sticks, flowers, stones, and other objects you find. As you find objects, arrange them in your painting again, letting your intuition guide you into how to depict your story.

When you're finished, sit and observe your nature painting. What do you notice about the objects you chose and how you arranged them? For example, observe whether your painting is symmetrical and balanced or objects are clustered in one part of the painting. Maybe you put delicate objects, like leaves or flower petals, in one spot and sturdier objects, like stones, in another. Think metaphorically about the positions of objects in relation to each other: Perhaps they're separated from each other because you tend to compartmentalize? If you chose seed pods instead of sticks, leaves, or stones to make your painting, maybe that tells you something about what you want to grow or what has potential not yet realized.

What I notice about the objects in my nature painting: _____

_____

_____

_____

_____

Next, ask your wise inner self, *What does this nature painting tell me about this part of my story*? Don't try to figure out its meaning. Let your intuitive mind—your wise inner self—guide you in interpreting the meaning.

My nature painting tells me: _____

_____

_____

_____

_____

_____

_____

_____

Here are some insights your wise inner self might give you as you sit before your painting, intuiting its meaning:

- *I have so much going on that I'm not focused on what is most important to me.*

- *I don't feel supported in making changes in my story.*

- *I go into denial about what's bothering me, and I want to be more honest with myself.*

Draw your nature painting here if you like, or insert a printed-out photo that you take of the painting so that you can come back to it and better understand its meaning by using your intuition and consulting your wise inner self:

Once you've created a nature painting, you can let nature rearrange it over time and then come back to see if you have new insights into your story. For example, if the wind or animals cause certain items you placed on your painting to move or even disappear, what do you make of that? Every story is influenced by forces beyond our control. If you've come back to your painting to see how nature has changed it and to gain insights into what the new arrangement can tell you, you can write about it here.

Nature transformed my nature painting. Now, with the help of my wise inner self, I am observing the following changes to my painting and have the following insights about these changes and what they mean: _____

_____

_____

_____

_____

_____

_____

Once you've completed the exercises in this chapter, you'll have gained clarity about the new story you want to write consciously. Keeping in mind what you learned about one or two chapters of your life you wanted to work on, what you learned and experienced because of doing the nature painting and the two journeys, you might want to write out a new story that integrates all your new insights.

My new story is: _____

_____

_____

_____

_____

Remember, stories can change over time. The more work you do with this workbook, the more insights you'll have into what you want to experience. Your story is likely to continue to transform and expand.

Because you are working with your unconscious in the form of your wise inner self, you are also likely to gain fuel for change, which will make it easier to follow through on working toward any goals you set. In the next chapter, you will clarify your values, priorities, and goals and learn how to maximize your potential for living according to your new story.

Part II
Making Changes

Chapter 6
Know Your Values and Priorities and Be True to Them

How much of your story has involved yearning for something else? Maybe the job you thought you would love turned out to be very different from what you thought it would be. Or you found that special someone, but at some point, the reality of the other person emerged, and the match no longer seemed made in heaven. The way we deal with the intersection of reality and our idealized fantasies determines our happiness.

Buddhism teaches us that our suffering is caused by attachments—for example, our attachment to having our expectations met. Yearning for something we don't have can be painful. Accepting what is, being contented in the present moment, can help relieve our discomfort and disappointment. Once, I wrote the following poem, which expresses the problem I see with not releasing expectations about what we think should happen and how others should act.

EXPECTATIONS

Regrets, resentments, and fears
are conceived
when expectations
impregnate what is.

Maybe you've found yourself mired in yearning for something you don't have. But is it something you truly want—or did you talk yourself into desiring it, believing that if only you could have this experience, situation, or person in your life, your troubles would melt away? What you truly yearn for might not be the perfect romantic partner, job, or living situation but something that is close enough to your ideal. After all, perfection is elusive. We can choose to reframe our past, as you've learned, but also our present. By choosing to accept and appreciate what you have and where you are, you can free yourself from the suffering caused by continually seeking something better. Then, you'll probably find you're more patient as you pursue whatever it is you yearn for—and more flexible about the form it takes. Maybe you don't need to acquire the home on the beach you've longed to own because you find other ways to enjoy being close to nature and the ocean.

Whatever your yearnings are, let go of the expectations that make you unhappy. Then, take action to achieve what you desire. Accept that you may have to go through long stretches where your circumstances aren't what you'd like them to be. By working on changing your story or one of its chapters, you can better handle these situations. You can also use your present circumstances as opportunities to reconnect with your values and remember what's important to you. From there, you can set new goals instead of trying to escape your situation or feeling stuck and unhappy or telling yourself you can only be content if something changes. Imagine you could live according to a story in which yearning exists but so does satisfaction. It's possible.

Take one chapter of your story, one area of your life, that you identified earlier as dissatisfying. Write a list of three to five things that you find dissatisfying about it.

A chapter of my story I'm dissatisfied with and some things that make it dissatisfying:

1)

2)

3)

4)

5)

Now write a list of three to five things that you find satisfying about that chapter or area.

Some things I find satisfying about that particular chapter of my story:

1)

2)

3)

4)

5)

Our brains typically are biased toward what makes us unhappy, scared, or angry. As you look at the two lists you just made, check in with your feelings. Maybe you came up with an equal number of positives and negatives about your situation, but you feel more strongly about the negatives than you do the positives. Maybe now that you listed the positives, the negatives don't seem so strong in the bigger picture. What you value might not be influencing your feelings as much as your bias toward the negative is. Let's check in with your values before setting goals to change what isn't working for you in a chapter of your story or your story overall.

Identifying Your Values and Priorities, the Foundations of Your Goals

What are your deepest values? Choose a value or two you would like to write about. Then, give an example of when you have acted according to your values and when you have not. In this way, you can begin to see any conflicts between what you value and the choices you make. The values might include honesty, loyalty, kindness, compassion, playfulness, status, belonging, or something else.

One of my values and a time when I exhibited it and a time when I did not: _____

_____

_____

_____

_____

_____

Another of my values and a time when I exhibited it and a time when I did not: _____

_____

_____

_____

_____

_____

_____

As you look at the examples of times you lived up to your values and the times you did not, see if you have any insights. You might want to ask your wise inner self, *What can you tell me about the times when I lived up to this particular value?* and *What can you tell me about times when I did not live up to this particular value?*

Maybe you say you have certain values but when you're truly honest with yourself, you don't hold them as deeply as you think you do. How much have you examined the foundational values by which you're living your life? Try answering the questions below as a challenge to be honest with yourself about what you value. Although thinking about the following situation might feel frustrating or uncomfortable, it is a way to uncover your true core values.

Suppose you have enough water for you, your spouse or partner, and/or your children and pets to survive for six months. During this period, there's a 50-50 chance you'll be given more water—and you know the water supply will return in six months. Meanwhile, other people around you are dying of thirst, and they beg you for water.

Would you sacrifice water for them? Circle one: Yes No

What if the person asking was a good friend, a sibling, or a parent? Circle one: Yes No

Your thoughts on this ethical challenge: _____

_____

_____

_____

Maybe you resist the premise of this ethical challenge and hold onto the belief that there must be a creative solution that allows everyone to have water. Even though the choice posed in the above scenario is highly unlikely to materialize, working with it can help you see that loyalties can be divided. There are times when you must make difficult choices. Will your ideals and beliefs hold up in those situations?

Often, our beliefs and values have gone unchallenged. We live according to the same old story we always have, never reflecting on why we think, feel, and act as we do—unaware that we have the power to change our story to a better one. When someone we care about does something that brings our beliefs or values into question, we may revisit and struggle with what we believed or valued wholeheartedly for a lifetime. It may not have occurred to us that someday we would have to examine it.

Think about an unquestioned belief or value that you hold. Imagine a situation that would cause you to question it. How might your belief or value change? For example, most people value honesty and condemn stealing. If someone you love told you that they had done something unethical, such as stealing something small, and wanted you to keep their secret, would your feelings and beliefs about honesty change? Whatever situation you choose, it should be one that involves a conflict between your values and someone else's or between two values you hold, such as honesty and loyalty to others or kindness and social justice. Consider writing here about the imagined situation and how your beliefs might or might not change and what you would do.

A situation that would cause me to question my beliefs—and my thoughts about what I would do if that situation became a reality: _____

_____

_____

_____

_____

_____

_____

Freeing Up Energy

One of the requirements for becoming a Jungian analyst is to undergo personal analysis, a type of therapy popularized by Sigmund Freud and Carl Jung. In the beginning, I committed to doing it mostly because I had to in order to fulfill my goal. I soon learned, though, how valuable the analytic process was. As I did the work, I made an important discovery: I had used a lot of energy to keep myself unaware of aspects of myself I found shameful or embarrassing. I had many distractions to keep me busy and to help me avoid feeling insecure, angry, or sad.

In allowing myself to become aware of my feelings, I began to free up energy that I could use for other things. I became even busier than I had been! Remaining busy became an act of defense because it kept me from further self-exploration that might distress me. Analysis was difficult enough, I rationalized. I didn't want random regrets, unexplained irritability, or other challenging emotional experiences to pop up suddenly. I liked the idea of containing my exploration to my therapy sessions. That was easier to accomplish when I extended my to-do list and kept myself busy and distracted.

In retrospect, I would have been better served by contemplating how to use my energy differently to serve myself, Spirit, and those I cared about. A vacuum of time is quickly filled, and I found plenty of activities to keep me from the challenging work of changing my life to be more in sync with my values. I didn't take time out to assess what I really wanted to be doing. It seemed the to-do list filled itself up on its own.

A friend of mine keeps his to-do list in a computer file, and every time he completes a task, he deletes an item on the list. When he thinks of something else he ought to do, he adds it to the list. Every day, he wakes up to an agenda that never seems to grow shorter, only longer. He does not have an entry for *whittle down my to-do list* or *contemplate what I most want to do with my time.*

You might want to look at your own to-do list and identify an item or two that you could discard, and then answer the following questions.

If there are any items you want to cross off your to-do list, what are they? _____

_____

_____

_____

_____

Look at the items at the top of your list. Why are they at the top? _____

_____

_____

_____

As you look at the list, have you prioritized what you say you value, and if not, why do you think that is? _____

_____

_____

_____

Remaining continually busy can keep you from self-exploration that might distress you but that also might help you live more authentically, with a greater sense of control over your life and more in synch with your priorities.

Contemplation and Self-Discovery

Even when contemplation is uncomfortable, it's worth tolerating that feeling so you can discover what your conscious mind is avoiding. It may be emotions you need to explore, learn from, and release. It may be insights that make you sad or angry but also push you to change. Only if you take time to discover and understand the uncomfortable aspects of yourself and your life can you begin to make important changes and live with more satisfaction and a greater sense of control over your story.

Think about how much time you spend being still and allowing hidden thoughts and feelings to arise in your awareness. Spend some time being contemplative and pondering your choices, experiences, and story. You might be underestimating how much energy and courage you have to face your challenges. What could you do to carve out more time for contemplation and self-discovery, and what goal are you willing to set for yourself?

If you'd like to set a specific goal and hold yourself accountable to it, you can do so here.

Keeping in mind the need for accountability, I'm setting this specific, achievable goal for contemplation and self-discovery: _____

_____

_____

I achieved my goal: Yes No (Circle one)

Any notes on what helped or hindered me in trying to reach my goal: _____

_____

_____

_____

_____

Your Story of Happiness

Earlier I said your story has chapters on health, relationships, psychology, and more. You might also think of happiness as a chapter in the story of your life. Is your happiness chapter's story something like: *I deserve to be happy and that means making time to have fun* or *Doing things I love is good for my health and well-being, so I make sure to do them*?

If it doesn't seem important to do what makes you happy because you've told yourself you're happy enough, you might want to question that belief. Do you have a happiness story such as, *It's selfish to take time for myself* or *Other people's needs are more important than what I'd like to do with my time*? Maybe you resist making time for what you enjoy because growing up, you regularly received the message that good people work hard all day long and are constantly productive. That internalized message of "all work and no play" can color your perception of how much time you should devote to simply having fun. For parts of my life, I felt that I and others around me shouldn't play until the chores were done. The chores list was endless, and I eventually learned that holding off on enjoyment until I felt I had finished all my tasks wasn't a good way to live.

You might have adopted a story about happiness that was written by someone else. If you were taught that what you enjoy isn't all that important, taking a Journey to the Room of Contracts to Change a Hidden Belief might help you adopt new beliefs that lead to greater happiness. Also, a dialogue with your wise inner self can help you to determine what you'd like your happiness story to be, although you may already have a sense of what you'd like it to be. Whatever the case, you can write your happiness story here.

I would like my happiness story to be: _____

_____

_____

_____

_____

If I used a hidden-wisdom technique to learn more about my happiness and my story about it, this is what I experienced and learned: _____

_____

_____

_____

_____

Often, we think if we can just have more money or a particular set of circumstances, we will be happy. These kinds of attachments can cause us a great deal of pain, as I wrote about in the following poem:

WANTING

The pain of wanting
can fester and kill
when what is wanted
cannot be.

But when the bearer of desire
shines the light of eternity onto the wanting
it transforms into a mirror that reflects the truth
and heals.

Happiness is easier to attain if we're willing to make changes to ourselves and our lives rather than hoping for other people and external circumstances to change.

Making Difficult Changes

It's said that the longest journey starts with one step, but sometimes that step seems so big that we talk ourselves out of taking it. We fear uncertainty and the risk that change may cause us to become less happy and fulfilled than we are now.

I check off the easy items on my to-do list and take a long time to get to the hard ones. I tell myself, *I don't have enough time or energy today, so I'll wait.* But I've learned that hard things can be broken down into smaller tasks that are easier for me to tackle. If I start at the margins of a big task and work my way in toward the center, eventually I'm able to do the hard things, even though I was reluctant to start them because they seemed overwhelming.

We all like to feel busy and that we are doing something worthwhile. But the tough problems don't seem to get solved when we distract ourselves with the easy tasks.

Sometimes we must make painful choices now to minimize the chance that down the road, we will have to make choices that are even more painful. And sometimes, even when a good solution is found, the process of change is painful and frightening, which leads to resistance.

Maybe you resist taking action because you think you need to gather more information or get input from others who have faced similar circumstances. Maybe you don't know how you feel about what you'll experience if you make the change. If so, what could you do to take a first step today toward gathering more information or input so you can both gain clarity on what step to take next and feel your resistance reducing?

I could take this first step today: _____

_____

_____

_____

_____

Again, if you can't figure out the answer, consult your wise inner self and dialogue with it. This way, possibilities you haven't considered can arise in your awareness.

Consider spending a little bit of time tackling the tough problems every day. If you take the first step today, you'll start to feel better about yourself and your situation. As you address your toughest problems, you'll develop competence and a sense of agency, and you won't have as many weighty things hanging over your head day after day.

While your wise inner self can be very helpful in changing your story and writing a new, more satisfying one, it's also good to know more about practical ways to change stubborn habits. We'll look at those strategies next.

Chapter 7
Pause and Become Mindful

Throughout this workbook, you've been learning how to gain insights about yourself by working with your hidden wisdom. You've also discovered how to access energy for transformation. To experience a shift, you need to slow down your responses to stressful situations and people instead of being highly reactive to them. You want to practice mindfulness—being fully present in the moment instead of worrying about the past or future. And you want to take pauses so you can observe what's happening, including any emotions and thoughts you're having. Practicing greater self-awareness and taking time to self-reflect will be extremely helpful for changing how you interact with others and how you frame your experiences.

Let's start with a simple mindfulness practice of appreciation.

Become Mindful Through Observing and Appreciating Moments

The Japanese have a term, *awaremu*, for the sublime moment of perfection just before the experience fades. Sometimes translated as sensitivity or awareness, *awaremu* is often used when referring to the beauty of cherry blossoms in full bloom. Of course, the cherry trees will blossom again next year, but the distractions of everyday life can cause us to forget to slow down and enjoy them. We assume we will see them again, but there's no way to know for sure that we will.

It's easy to let our minds wander and forget to focus on the sweetness of an experience, on the pleasures that life offers us here and there in moments of perfection. However, if we're too distracted to notice these moments, we may find ourselves missing out on sublime living. Are you choosing to observe moments of perfection as opposed to rushing through life? You might learn something about yourself if you slow down to practice awaremu.

Think about the last moments you have experienced, a time when you watched the sun set and experienced the last moment before the sun dipped below the horizon. Think about the moment before a seed leaves the dandelion, taken away on the wind. Think about the moment you experience every morning before you open your eyes to a new day. Every day is filled with last moments like this, some of which you might be aware of, some of which pass without your notice. Similar moments may come again, but you might not take the time to appreciate them and be fully present with them. You miss them because they seem too ordinary to be worthy of your attention.

Why bother observing these moments? Because any ordinary moment can become extraordinary due to something that happens or because you experience it as beyond the mundane. You might realize as you open your eyes one morning that given the fragility of life, you are fortunate to experience another day. You might make a choice to be mindful of that last moment, or you might find yourself doing it naturally. If you made a conscious choice to experience that moment of awakening as one in which to feel grateful that you are alive, maybe the moment would have more meaning for you. Then, maybe you would come to be more aware of what you want to experience before you close your eyes to fall asleep at the end of the day. Mindfulness helps us to stay on track with living according to a new story we have written that we want to experience. It keeps us from falling back into old habits and old dissatisfying patterns.

Mindfulness helps us to stay on track with our goals and live according to a new story we have written that we want to experience.

Answering the following questions might help you live more consciously and wisely.

Is there something you would do differently today if you knew this were your last chance to have that experience, and if so, what is it? _____

_____

_____

_____

When you do experience pleasure, are you fully conscious of that experience before it gives way to the next experience, and if not, why not? _____

_____

_____

You might want to make a point of observing a sunset so that you pause to take in the colors, light, and clouds. As you see the colors changing and the clouds moving, realize that one moment is giving way to another until there is one last moment before the sun sets completely. Pay attention to how you feel and what thoughts come up for you. As one moment passes, and then another, you might want to ask yourself, *What if this were the last sunset I would see?* Notice whether it's easier to appreciate this experience when you pretend it will be the last time you have it. Then reflect on the experience, answering these questions.

What if any emotions and thoughts came up for you during this experience? For example, did thinking about this being the last sunset you would see bring up any insights about how youarespendingyourtime?_____

_____

_____

_____

Next, you might watch a seed such as a dandelion, maple, or cottonwood seed carried on the wind, remaining present in the moment as it flies about. Then, as its path changes, notice that in the blink of an eye, your moment of observation has already become part of the past. The seed will never be in the same place again. You will never again experience this moment that is passing. Now think about experiences in your life that may seem ordinary but that you are certain you would like to have again. What are some of them?

I would like to again experience: _____

_____

_____

_____

The more you focus on what gives you joy and makes you feel vitalized, and on what makes you feel a sense of purpose or meaning, the easier it will be to change your priorities and let go of the plotlines and events that seem scripted by someone else. You'll find it easier to rearrange items on your to-do list as you recognize the importance of enjoying the sunrise or sunset or taking the extra time to listen to a friend or loved one in need of attention.

When you practice mindfulness, you'll more easily recognize sublime simple moments. Mindfulness gives us greater control over our lives: our thoughts, emotions, responses to the world, and actions. It also helps us to remember our spiritual nature—and that we have hidden wisdom we can tap into. The more mindful we are, the easier it is to set aside distractions and hear the messages our hidden wisdom is sending us, which in turn helps us make choices based on our values.

While you might not think it's important to be mindful of small moments, consider this: Often when someone dies, we immediately think back to the last time we saw them. What would we have done differently had we known that this was our last moment with them? Sometimes, we sense we are experiencing a last moment, a final good-bye—for example, when a person we know is in a dying process. We hope to see them again but are aware that we might not. We can never know when the last moment is, but if we make a point of being fully present with people regardless of whether or not they are seriously ill, we may find ourselves having fewer regrets about our actions.

Think about this: Some moment you think of as ordinary will end up being the last such moment. Knowing that might make it easier for you to appreciate the time you have left on this earth and to work with it more consciously instead of allowing distractions and hidden patterns to determine what your life will be like. Becoming mindful of the moment helps you experience fewer regrets. That's because you'll have been more aware of the decisions you are making about how to spend your limited number of moments on this earth.

Discover the Potential for Change in One Short Pause

Sometimes, one short pause holds potential for a big positive transformation even if the situation we're in doesn't look promising. By not instantly reacting with pessimism and instead, taking your time to be fully present with your feelings in the moment, you free yourself to shift perspective. That shift might be a profound one. Taking one short pause here and there to check in with your hidden wisdom is a form of mindfulness.

If something doesn't feel right, a short pause can awaken your ability to hear your hidden wisdom telling you why that's the case. Then, you can make a conscious decision instead of responding automatically as you normally would. You might have a pattern of walking away from relationships when they become boring to you or because you feel an urge to leave and you don't quite know why. By taking a pause to reflect, you can avoid leaving one situation only to find you end up in a similar one, feeling just as uneasy as you were the last time and about to fall back into old habits you wanted to change.

If something doesn't feel right, a short pause can awaken your ability to hear your hidden wisdom telling you why that's the case.

Pause to Reflect on How You Make Decisions

A pause gives you a chance to reflect not just on what happened and what others did but on your own choices. You can reflect on whether there were other choices you could have made and why you didn't make them. You can learn more about your decision-making process. It might be a process that works well for you in some situations but not others, or it might be problematic for you in many situations. It might even be one that doesn't work well for you and needs to be replaced by a better one.

When making decisions, we should be aware of the potential for, as T.S. Eliot wrote in his poem *The Waste Land*, "The awful daring of a moment's surrender, Which an age of prudence can never retract." Maybe you've made a decision you have come to regret. Perhaps you were too impulsive and, if you had given yourself a pause for reflection, your choice might have been different. Even if you had come to the same conclusion, a pause would have allowed your hidden wisdom to speak to you. Then, because your decision came from a deeper level of awareness, you might not regret the choice or second-guess yourself.

Sometimes we make rash decisions out of habit or because we want to make our choice based on what others want. When that happens, we can start to doubt whether the path we took was the best one for us.

In some situations, surrendering in the moment may have been exactly the right thing for you to have done, but who is to say? I don't regret becoming a businessman. I was good at it, and it allowed me to develop enough financial security to support my family. But my decision to study something I felt was practical instead of psychology, which I was very interested in, was not just based on my impression that some psychologists seemed a little crazy! It was also based on what my family and community expected of a man like me. I never took a pause to ask myself, Is a practical field of study what I truly want? And if so, how do I know that's the case? Later, I was able to study psychology, but in some cases, the decisions you make close off possibilities for you that you'll come to regret are no longer there.

Think about a decision you made that led to an outcome you are not sure is the one you most wanted. Pause to reflect on your feelings about that decision and how you made it. Remember, your decision might not have been an entirely conscious one, so don't be hard on yourself if you feel you should have known better or spent more time making your decision and exploring your feelings. If you like, you can do a dialogue with your hidden wisdom to learn more about why you made the decision and see what you learn about any unconscious influences on your decision making.

A decision of mine that led to an outcome I either don't like or is not what I most wanted:

_____

_____

_____

_____

I now can see that my decision-making process in that situation was: _____

_____

_____

_____

_____

If your decision-making process was rushed, you might want to try to slow down when you are faced with decisions. The words *let me get back to you on that* and *I haven't decided yet* can be empowering.

Pause to Reflect on Your Role in a Situation

Often people get into the habit of blaming situations or other people for their unhappiness but don't look at their own role in what happened. Taking a short pause to self-reflect can help you to see what part you played, however small, in bringing about an outcome you didn't like. Then, you can dialogue with your hidden wisdom to learn more about your role in the situation and whether you're contented with it. Maybe you'll find that you want to apologize to someone, or maybe you'll find you wish you would have asserted yourself instead of giving into the other person's wishes. It can be especially helpful to reflect on the part you played in any conflicts, being compassionate toward yourself as you look back at the choices you made. Learning more about yourself and your habits is the first step in making more conscious decisions, so give yourself credit for doing the challenging work of reflecting on your role in situations that didn't yield your preferred outcome.

Think about a situation you are in or have been in recently that was frustrating or upsetting, one in which you can see how someone else's behavior was a problem for you. Step back from the notion of blame to see how one thing you did either made the situation worse or didn't help it to be more satisfying and pleasant. If you feel embarrassed, ashamed, or resistant, remember that when we don't recognize that there are other choices we can make, we have a harder time shifting situations than if we are able to see different options. Reflecting on a choice or choices you made can help you make ones in the future that lead to better outcomes.

Be compassionate toward yourself as you look back at choices you made.

My role, however small, in a frustrating or upsetting situation I recently experienced was:

_____

_____

_____

What I could have done instead that might have been a better choice for me: _____

_____

_____

_____

Pause to Make an Inner Shift

A pause can also be used to refresh yourself and change your mood, outlook, and energy. When you're feeling frazzled, you can take a short pause to focus on your breathing, slowly inhaling and exhaling while tuning into the sensation of your breathing. By breathing in for four counts, holding your breath for seven, and exhaling for eight counts—that is, using the 4-7-8 breathing technique created by Dr. Andrew Weil—you cue your parasympathetic nervous system to activate and relax you. That helps you release any anxiety. Take a pause now to try it: Breathe in for a count of four, hold your breath for a count of seven, and exhale for a count of eight. Try it again a few times. Notice how much more relaxed you feel.

Letting go of fear and worry helps you shift into a more optimistic and hopeful mood, particularly if you also use the short pause to assert something positive. For example, you could release your fear and worry with the 4-7-8 breathing technique and say to yourself, *This too shall pass*, or *I'll be okay. I know I will*, or *Let it go*. Continue taking short pauses in this way and you might find you're developing a new habit of being more positive about your present and future.

Some things I can do or say to myself during short pauses to shift my mood or state of mind are: _____

_____

_____

_____

_____

_____

Pause to Connect with Nature

Time in nature can strongly support physical and mental wellness, so taking a short pause to reconnect with the earth and her elements, creatures, and plants can start you on the road to greater health and well-being. You can take a short pause to connect with nature, even if just in your own mind. Picture a place in nature and imagine yourself there, immersed in the sensory experience as you watch the clouds pass in front of the moon or observe the wind rippling the surface of a pond or lake. If you can go outside into nature, take a short pause to observe a bee drawing nectar from a flower or the movement of a creek as it tumbles over rocks. A few minutes in nature might help you recognize that you are under a lot of stress lately and need to take time out to relax. You might realize you need to get out into nature more often and let it soothe you.

And time in nature can help you learn its lessons, feel more connected to Spirit, and recalibrate—because nature can make our problems seem less overwhelming. You'll learn more about nature and its benefits in Chapter 13: Connecting with Your Spirituality and with Nature.

What I could do to feel more connected to nature is: _____

_____

_____

_____

_____

Taking a short pause to reconnect with the earth and her elements, creatures, and plants can start you on the road to greater health and well-being.

Having become more mindful and observant, you're less likely to respond to other people and to situations in ways you'll regret, reducing how often you get hurt or you hurt others with your words and actions. Next, we'll look at practical ways to establish new habits that will support better relationships.

Chapter 8
Take Wise Action to Establish New Habits

Now it's time to start taking wise actions toward attaining the changes you decided you want to make. If you find yourself stuck, procrastinating, or frustrated by an obstacle, remember that your hidden wisdom can probably shed light on what's happening within you that you might not be aware of, such as a hidden resistance to change. Your hidden wisdom can be enormously helpful in keeping you on track and accountable to yourself, even when it seems the problem with moving forward is external. Hidden wisdom will also help you write new, more satisfying stories and bring them to life.

New Habits Start with Achievable Goals and Accountability

The trick to acquiring new habits and ridding yourself of old ones is to set achievable, well-defined goals. If you want to save money for retirement or a special trip, could you save a little every week—perhaps five or ten dollars to start, with the aim of increasing the amount later? If you want to have fewer aches and pains, and you often wait for an elevator, you might get into the habit of stretching your calves or shoulder muscles until the elevator shows up. It's a small practice that will make you a little more limber and that can be amplified by doing it more often and in more situations.

To live according to the new story you wrote in Chapter 5, identify some new habits, however small, that will help you bring it to life and feel that you are not just doing what is expected of you but what you want to do. Maybe you want to get in the habit of devoting the first three hours after breakfast every Saturday morning to working on a creative project that's important to you. Maybe to achieve better health, you want to establish the habit of walking regularly for exercise. You might want to start doing it for just five minutes a day to start. Again, make each goal simple, well-defined, and achievable, and set a deadline to reach it.

If you're not a creature of habit, pay attention to any habits you have that are automatic—that you didn't plan to establish. For example, you wake up in the morning—that's a habit even if

91

you awaken at different times on different days. You eat—maybe three times a day plus snacks or maybe more erratically. You use the bathroom, get into a car, or turn on your computer for the day, unplug your phone from its charger—we all have habits that may not occur at the same times each day, but they occur. Write a list of some of your daily habits here (such as brushing your teeth, getting out of bed in the morning, etc.), because it will be helpful to work with this list and hook a habit onto a habit, which you'll learn about shortly.

My daily habits include: _____

_____

_____

_____

_____

_____

_____

If you're now ready to set a new goal for yourself, and establish a new habit in the one or two chapters of your life where you most want to make a change, write it here. Remember to make it specific and give yourself accountability, as explained earlier.

Keeping in mind the need for accountability, I'm setting this specific, achievable goal for establishing a new habit: _____

_____

_____

I achieved my goal: Yes No (Circle one)

Any notes on what helped or hindered me in trying to reach my goal: _____

_____

_____

_____

_____

_____

One Healthy Change Leads to Another

Your desires, goals, and priorities can change over time. As you develop courage and confidence, you're likely to find yourself dreaming bigger and setting goals for changing areas of your life you used to think you couldn't possibly change. For example, you might come to believe you truly can rid yourself of some of the aches and pains you have that are related to aging or a physical condition. Developing greater physical strength and stamina might not seem so hard to achieve after all because you have new habits. On the other hand, you might decide you no longer want to work quite so hard on one chapter of your life. You might stop trying to add new goals and habits for improving your physical health and instead simply enjoy your body more—doing exercise, such as dancing, that is pleasurable rather than a chore. Alternatively, you might choose to focus on another chapter of your life now that you're satisfied with your physical habits.

Making changes in one area of your life might help you notice where else you need to make them. Often, one healthy change leads to another because you create momentum, develop confidence, and enjoy the new habit. As you start to exercise more, you might start to catch yourself eating less of the junk foods that you used to eat mindlessly. You might find you like walking for a few minutes while listening to music or your favorite podcast, so much so that you find yourself walking for even longer. If you meditate for five minutes before getting out of bed each morning, you might find yourself making other small changes, such as stretching more often during the day, because you can see how just a few minutes devoted to a new habit pays off.

Often, one healthy change leads to another because you create momentum, develop confidence, and enjoy the new habit.

Change is a part of life, and when we learn to make healthy changes, however small, we can start to establish new habits. We also remind ourselves that a transformation process doesn't have to be extremely difficult or deeply uncomfortable. In fact, it can be invigorating. Results such as being more fit because of changing your exercise habits, or feeling more energized in the morning, might motivate you to make even more changes.

Reflecting on your past successes at transformation can help you gain confidence as you strive to meet new goals. Take a minute now to write about your transition from struggling to success with a specific problem, however small. For example, maybe as a teenager you were nervous as you learned to drive. Maybe when you began your job, you were worried about the challenge of being at the beginning of some learning curves. All of us have successes in our past. Identify one of yours—perhaps the one you're most proud of, because it was the biggest challenge you ever overcame. Also, pay attention to how you feel as you write your story, acknowledging what you have done and experienced. The confidence and pride you feel as you reflect on this past success can be very motivating.

A story of my transition from struggle to success: _____

_____

_____

_____

_____

_____

_____

_____

_____

_____

You might want to consult your hidden wisdom about the success you achieved and write about. You can ask, *What insights do you have about the struggle I experienced and the success I ultimately achieved?* If you choose to release something energetically and bring in something new, let your hidden wisdom guide you on what that can be and what payoffs you'll receive. Perhaps you'll let go of your tendency to be too hard on yourself and forget about your successes—or your habit of telling yourself that your success was due mostly to luck. Perhaps you'll bring in the belief that your success at achieving one goal will serve you in achieving other ones even if they are very different. For example, you might think that being adept at adjusting to work challenges won't benefit you in changing your eating and exercise habits, but you could be very wrong about that. Your hidden wisdom's messages might boost your confidence far more than you would expect even as you receive insights and energy for change.

One healthy change often leads to another. In this way, incrementally, you can experience your ability to transform any aspect of your life.

Also, note any other changes you've experienced because you set and achieved a goal for transformation. You might want to write about how you feel about your success and how you attained it.

Anything I've learned and experienced so far as a result of pursuing and achieving my goal(s):

_____

_____

_____

_____

_____

If you're now ready to set a new goal for yourself in the one or two chapters of your life where you most want to make a change, so that you'll establish a new habit, write it here.

Keeping in mind the need for accountability, I'm setting this specific, achievable goal for myself: _____

_____

_____

_____

I achieved my goal: Yes No (Circle one)

Any notes on what helped or hindered me in trying to reach my goal: _____

_____

_____

_____

If you didn't succeed at reaching your aim, don't worry—and don't give up. You can try again if you like, perhaps revising the goal slightly if you believe that will help you overcome any obstacles to achieving it.

Making New Habits Stick

When you consult your hidden wisdom about the changes you want to make, you might feel a shift as you release energy you no longer need and receive energy and insights that serve you. When encountering your hidden wisdom during a meditative session as described earlier, you might want to experiment with reaching your arms out in a gesture of releasing something to your wise inner self who is in front of you—or drawing in your arms to accept and pull into yourself whatever your wise inner self is giving you. I have found that these movements can be helpful for feeling an energetic shift that gives me momentum to follow through on making changes, adopting habits that stick.

There are other ways to get a new habit to stick, too. You learned about one, which is setting concrete, well-defined goals with a specific date attached to them. Here are some more to keep in mind.

Hook a Habit onto a Habit

Use your existing habits, which you identified earlier in this chapter, to your advantage. It's easier to make new habits stick if you combine them with old ones. Every morning, you get out of bed. Every time you sit down for a meal, you pull out a chair. Those are just two examples of habits you probably have already. Go back to the list you made earlier and figure out which habits you can most easily hook your new habit onto. For example, you could choose to do a light stretching routine every morning when you get out of bed. Before you take your seat at your table for a meal, you can take a moment to silently acknowledge your gratitude for having food to eat.

If you brush your teeth after breakfast each day, could you commit to doing something else, such as three minutes of stretching and yoga, right after you finish brushing? If on Thursdays, you have a fun evening class, could you come home from class, log into your bank account, and transfer ten dollars from your checking to your savings, hooking your habit of saving to your habit of going to class?

Before you write below about some habits you know you would like to establish, you might want to look back at the list of habits you wrote a few pages ago to see which ones you can hook new habits onto.

Habits I'd like to establish and some existing habits I could hook them onto: _____

_____

_____

_____

_____

_____

_____

_____

Make Your New Habit Convenient

Our minds like to work on autopilot. It's easier to make the small choice that leads to your goal if it's convenient to do so. Keep your gym bag packed and in your car, don't buy wine to keep at home if you'd like to reduce your wine drinking, or find some other way to make the new habit you want to adopt very easy to follow through on.

Ways I could make it more convenient to establish a new habit: _____

_____

_____

_____

_____

_____

_____

If you'd like to set a goal for establishing a new habit, you can write it down here and make a note on your calendar to check in with yourself to see if you've made progress toward your goal. Whether or not you achieve it, you might want to explore what happened so that you learn a little more about yourself and what does and doesn't work for achieving goals.

Keeping in mind the need for accountability, I'm setting this specific, achievable goal for establishing a new habit: _____

_____

_____

_____

I achieved my goal: Yes No (Circle one)

Any notes on what helped or hindered me in trying to reach my goal: _____

_____

_____

_____

_____

Give Yourself Structure *and* Flexibility

It's important to have some structure regarding your goals—for example, you're going to take certain actions. It's also important to be flexible. Without flexibility, you're more likely to give up on establishing new habits.

Some people are very rigid, always striving to do better, never letting up on themselves. They may achieve excellence in more than one chapter of their life, but is their intensity worth the cost? The stress of feeling you must always accomplish more and never let up on improving your life can take its toll. How can you know you need more flexibility regarding goals and more compassion for yourself?

You're having health issues related to stress. Maybe you are experiencing symptoms of a condition that is under control on the rare occasions when you lighten up—for example, when you're on vacation. Chronic stress leads to low-grade inflammation. That in turn leads to aging before your time and developing any number of diseases. While you may be on top of medical appointments, nutritional interventions to reduce symptoms of a disease, and the latest research on how you can be healthier, you might be deceiving yourself about how much stress you cause yourself by trying to be perfect or letting your inner drive take over your life.

You are regularly irritable and inflexible. If you are short-tempered and closed off to suggestions that you relax more, reduce stress, and make time for downtime, it's likely that you need to make some changes. If your friends and family members have been telling you to lighten up and go with the flow more often, be honest with yourself about whether you are listening to them or minimizing their observations. Being rigid and difficult puts a strain on yourself but also on your relationships. Stop for a few moments to reflect on any warning signs you have received about your irritability and inflexibility.

You are continually missing the mark even when you set specific goals with deadlines. It's possible that you have to learn more about how to maximize your success at changing habits and reaching your aims, but maybe part of you isn't truly committed. That can be hard to admit, so dialoguing with your hidden wisdom to learn more might be a good idea. You can use the dialoguing method or make a nature painting to learn more. You might make the painting about your commitment to your goals that you keep failing to achieve. See what the leaves, twigs, stones, and feathers you find and arrange reveal to you—what message from hidden wisdom they bear as a result of your intuitive selecting and placing of the items in your painting.

Do you have a plan for days, or even weeks, when sticking with your goal is likely to be especially difficult? Your hidden wisdom might offer you some insights into staying the course that you might not figure out on your own. You might want to dialogue with your wise inner self or use another hidden-wisdom technique to learn more. If you choose to do that, you can write about your experience here.

My experience using a hidden-wisdom technique to learn more about being flexible regarding goals was this: _____

_____

_____

_____

_____

_____

_____

_____

_____

Then too, by observing any changes you have experienced because of setting and achieving a goal, you can learn from your own experiences. Below, you can reflect on your successes.

What I have learned about myself when it comes to establishing new habits: _____

_____

_____

_____

_____

It's possible that you have to learn more about how to maximize your success at changing habits and reaching your aims, but maybe part of you isn't truly committed to your goals.

If you couldn't achieve your goal, the key to success might actually be to set a goal to engage in the new behavior every day and then reward yourself if you did it at least five out of the seven days. Perfection isn't realistic, after all. Also, try to figure out what happened on those days that you didn't follow through. You might gain some valuable insights into how to take action when your plans are disrupted. If you didn't do a relaxing breathing exercise or meditation at lunchtime as you intended because an unexpected call came in, you could figure out a backup time when you could make up for any missed sessions.

My plan for having a little flexibility when establishing a new habit that I'd like to make stick:

_____

_____

_____

_____

_____

_____

Hold Yourself Accountable

Having a specific date by which you'll accomplish a goal is one way of holding yourself accountable for meeting it, but it's not the only way. If you wouldn't want to tell a friend that once again, you didn't follow through on doing what you said you would, you might ask them to check in with you at the end of the week to ask how you did. The potential embarrassment of having to admit that you didn't meet your goal could incentivize you.

A plan for a small reward when you meet a small goal can keep you from finding excuses not to take the actions you promised to take so you could establish a new habit. You might want to have a plan for rewarding yourself not just for reaching big goals but small ones. If you can tackle your project four Saturdays in a row or alter your bedtime or mealtime routine every day for two weeks, have a reward in mind for that accomplishment. But also stop to reward yourself after making a small but significant choice that takes you toward a larger goal. For example, if your goal is to update your resume and you've been putting it off for months but finally follow through, you might want to celebrate that in some way. What might seem easy to one person can be difficult for another depending on what their obstacles are. Your hidden wisdom can alert you to hidden resistance that, once it's made conscious, subsides enough that you achieve your goal at last.

Another way to hold yourself accountable is to set a timer to go off when you're supposed to engage in your new habit rather than, say, vaguely promising yourself to start that new decluttering-the-house routine first thing this Saturday. You can also note on your calendar that you've successfully made a small choice that can be one in a series of them that leads to a change in habits. Use a chart or checklist to help you keep track of your actions, marking your calendar or a chart whenever you meet your goal. You might want to pause to let yourself feel good about your choice and enjoy a sense of accomplishment when you mark your calendar, chart, or checklist. You can remind yourself of the progress you've made each time you gaze at the evidence that you are on your way to the big change you want to experience.

My thoughts on what might work to help me be more accountable to my goals: _____

_____

_____

_____

_____

_____

_____

Be Mindful at Choice Points

The choices we make are the stepping-stones on the way to transformation, but even when the way forward is clear, we can find ourselves stumbling on the path. If we can make the most of those moments of little choices, we'll have a far better chance of making big changes. Change requires a series of decisions you must make in the moment, ones that might not seem all that consequential at the time. You might tell yourself you'll watch just one more episode of an entertainment series or wait one more weekend before you get serious about a project you say you want to tackle. You might tell yourself, *I'll have just one bite* or *just one glass of wine tonight,* but do you find yourself saying you'll break your rule *just this once* yet doing it again and again? Check in with yourself at moments of choice to make sure you're not making small decisions you'll regret or neglecting to make choices you've vowed to make. If you find yourself tempted to make a one-time decision to ignore your opportunity to establish and reinforce a new habit, pause briefly to practice mindfulness. You can then ask yourself, *Why am I resisting going along with my plan? What's going on?* Simply experiencing a little relaxation and identifying why you're resistant can help you find the willpower to say to yourself, *This time, despite my resistance, I'm going to make the small choice I promised I would make in situations like this.*

Check in with yourself at moments of choice to make sure you're not making small decisions you'll regret or neglecting to make choices you've vowed to make.

If you're not meeting your new goals and establishing new habits, the next chapter can help.

Chapter 9
If You're Not Meeting Your Goals

Sometimes, we make the seemingly wrong small decision again and again at moments of choice because we aren't truly dedicated to the goal we set.

Maybe it's not big change you seek but "good enough" change. Maybe when you achieve your "good enough" change, you'll set a new, even bigger goal—but maybe you'll be satisfied with the decision you made to stop when you hit your mark. Either way, the more consciously you approach big changes, the more dedicated you will be to making the series of small changes needed to bring about transformation. You'll also be more satisfied and less likely to hold yourself to impossible standards or insist on maintaining unrealistic goals for yourself.

Once you find yourself establishing a new habit, such as doing three minutes of stretching or yoga after brushing your teeth each morning, or transferring a few dollars to your savings account every week, you might want to set a new goal that will bring you even closer to the larger one of changing a habit. For example, you might increase the number of minutes you spend stretching or doing yoga or increase the amount you put into your savings each week. You could also come up with a complementary goal. For example, once you start walking 500 steps a day consistently, you could increase that number to 650 but also add a minute or two of stretching. You could transfer another few dollars to your savings account each week and set a goal to evaluate subscriptions a couple of times a year to see if there is one you aren't using and could cancel, using the money instead to increase your savings.

If you fail to meet a goal, don't be hard on yourself and let your disappointment stop you from recommitting to transformation. Reflect on how you got off track. Then, address the problems. If you do meet your aim, pay attention to what strategies worked for you, as this workbook has encouraged you to do. Give yourself credit for the success but also for learning about what keeps you persevering. Be proud of having pushed yourself to meet your goal, however small it was. You've made one good change that stuck, and it's important to reinforce that success. You can now set a new goal toward accomplishing the larger, more abstract one, such as being more in touch with your emotions, or you can set a new goal for another chapter of your life.

Failing at reaching goals can be daunting. Too often, our default is to give up. Pessimism about possibilities offers some comfort, which is why we can find ourselves thinking, *I have to accept that I'm destined to be stuck in a low-paying job* or *I'll never find the time to learn how to sing, and anyway, what's the point? I probably have no talent.* But those thoughts won't get you to where you say you want to be.

In brief moments, you might feel the pain of longing, but without the courage to risk trying to reach your goal despite the possibility of failure, you might decide that abandoning hope is the sensible, safe thing to do. Maybe it is. Maybe you'll never make more money and have a job you love, but you can't know that. Maybe you'll never be a great singer. But who knows what your life could look like if you were to pursue your passion?

Have you started on the road to what you want to achieve only to lose momentum? Have you stalled out on the way to a goal? If so, and it's bothering you, maybe it's time to access your unconscious and remove any blocks to success that are hidden from your awareness.

Do Your Goals Match Your Values?

If your habits aren't working for you, and you believe you're doing your best to change them, you may be trying too hard to fix them using willpower instead of drawing on your hidden wisdom to guide and motivate you. Deep down, you might know that your goals don't match your values. Take spending habits: You might have objects in your home that you eagerly anticipated owning but that now inspire guilt when you look at them. If what you purchased did not provide you value after all, it's a sign that your spending habits aren't working for you. Similarly, you might say you value spending time with your family and friends, but if you're not prioritizing it, maybe you need to change your habits to be in sync with your values.

Very often, what we say we value and what we truly value are at odds with each other because there's a conflict between the conscious mind and the unconscious one, where hidden wisdom and knowledge reside. Maybe you don't actually want to spend more time with your family and friends because you highly value your solitude but are reluctant to admit to yourself much less anyone else that you often don't feel like socializing. Maybe you buy exercise equipment to overcome the worry that you're not going to follow through on your goal to exercise more. By purchasing a yoga mat and a rowing machine, you felt you were proving to yourself that you were truly committed, yet even so, you didn't follow through with your goal. Such inconsistencies are common. The key is to resolve them through being honest with yourself. A good way to do that is by self-reflecting and consulting your hidden wisdom.

Very often, what we say we value and what we truly value are at odds with each other because there's a conflict between the conscious mind and the unconscious one.

We tend to expend time and money on what we most value. You might want to identify some habits you have regarding time and money and explore whether they align or clash with your values. For example, shopping online at night when you're bored or spending a lot of time scrolling on your phone might not fit with your values.

One of my habits of spending time or money that doesn't fit with my values: _____

_____

_____

_____

_____

Some of my deepest values, as I discovered through the work in Chapter 6: _____

_____

_____

_____

_____

A way I spend time or money that aligns with my deepest values: _____ _____

_____

_____

_____

_____

Chances are that your wisest expenditures of time and money were on things that gave you emotional experiences you value. Maybe you took vacations or staycations at home where you devoted time to being with people you love and enjoying their company, engaging in simple pleasures, or reconnecting with yourself and your spirituality. Research shows we get more pleasure out of experiences and anticipating them than we do out of material objects, yet we continue to shop mindlessly.

Often when we spend money or time unwisely, we're looking for something that represents an experience we think only this expenditure can give us. What if you could have that experience a different way? For example, what if you could feel like an excellent cook without owning expensive cookware? What if you could feel confident and attractive without luxurious clothes and jewelry?

Look at objects in your home that you don't use but keep out of a sense of guilt or anticipation that someday, you'll use them. You can dialogue with an object you've attained—or with your hidden wisdom—to learn more about how you're spending your money or your time. If you do so, you can record your experience here.

What I learned and experienced dialoguing with an object to learn more about my values and how I spend my time and money: _____

_____
_____
_____
_____
_____
_____
_____
_____
_____

Feeling competent, loved, and admired, along with having a sense of belonging to a community, can best be achieved not by owning expensive tools for acquiring these experiences but by finding within yourself your competence, lovability, and worthiness of admiration and belonging. Journaling can help you explore why you believe you must buy something to experience these qualities. As you think about your spending habits, you might want to ponder these questions and write your answers to them.

What were the wisest expenditures of time and money that you ever made? What value did they bring to you? _____

_____
_____
_____
_____
_____

What is one way you could spend your time differently to achieve greater happiness and satisfaction? _____

_____

_____

_____

What is one way you could spend your money differently to achieve greater happiness and satisfaction? _____

_____

_____

_____

For you, money might have many meanings: success, security, freedom, power, and status, for example. With those associations in mind, what do you want your money story to be? For example, would it be something like *Money is for creating enough security that I feel okay with taking time away from work to be with family or enjoy my hobbies* or *I work hard to earn my money, so I want to spend it wisely*? See if you can identify your money story and time-spending story and new ones you would like to adopt.

The money story I seem to be living according to is: _____

_____

_____

The time-spending story I seem to be living according to is: _____

_____

_____

A money story I would like to adopt is: _____

_____

_____

A time-spending story I would like to adopt is: _____

_____

_____

Getting Unstuck

Some habits are like a sticky note, easily changed with conscious effort—usually, because they're new. More deeply engrained habits are typically more difficult to break.

The stickiness of our habits is imprinted in our brains' neural networks—highways between brain cells that information travels along. Each time we act according to an old pattern, we reinforce a neural network and the stickiness of the habit. Our brains are efficient at developing habits, but the brain's neural networks become like dirt paths worn into the ground by many feet crushing the grass and compacting the soil. We get stuck in a rut, taking the same paths again and again.

Sticky habits may no longer be serving you and can get in the way of establishing new, preferred habits. You don't necessarily have to get rid of your old habits altogether. You can reduce their energetic influence on you and change their qualities, so they affect you in a way that serves you better. Take mothering or fathering energy, which you can also think of as parenting energy. A mother often has a very hard time letting go of her old mothering habits after her children leave the nest. She may have very strong mothering energy that has established those habits. A father may have great difficulty not lecturing or advising his newly adult children when his fathering energy continues to be very strong. Even if you're not actually a parent, a strong parenting energy may be influencing the way you interact with others in ways that aren't working for you or them. By accessing your hidden wisdom, you can learn how you can relate differently to the archetypal energy of parenting and alter its effects on you.

You may need to release some of that archetypal energy into the energy field we all share and that connects us all. One way to reduce the strength of an archetypal energy that's affecting you is to close your eyes, focus on your breathing, and imagine yourself breathing out that archetypal energy on every exhalation. Imagine returning it to the greater energy field that connects us all, intending for it to be used for the highest good. Continue to breathe out the energy until you feel that much of its power has been released. Relax your muscles as you breathe in refreshing energy and as you exhale excess archetypal energy you don't need. In this way, you can start to loosen the grip of this archetypal energy, making it less sticky for you. Bit by bit, you can change the influence of archetypal energies on you and start to write and live according to a new story, one that is more pleasing to you and God or Spirit.

You may need to work with an archetypal energy to alter how you express it. For example, parenting energy can be expressed as nurturing, guiding, advising, and comforting others. If you confront your parenting energy in a dialogue to learn more from it, your hidden wisdom might make you aware of how you can be nurturing, serve as a guide or advisor, or comfort others in new ways. You might like to think you're expressing your parenting energy in all these ways for your children when you're actually stressing them out by being overbearing and controlling. You could express your parenting energy differently with them—and find others who appreciate your strong need to express this energy. Mentoring people, serving as a grandparent figure to children in the community, or nurturing and guiding a group that's devoted to a particular cause, whether it's for profit or not for profit, all can be satisfying, positive ways to express parenting energy.

You may need to work with an archetypal energy to alter how you express it.

If you decide to use a hidden-wisdom technique with the intention of encountering and working with an archetypal energy that can help you get unstuck, you might want to write about your experience here.

My experience using a hidden-wisdom technique to help me get unstuck: _____

_____

_____

_____

_____

_____

_____

_____

_____

_____

_____

One of the goals I've seen people struggle with is learning how to experience fewer conflicts and make those conflicts more productive. You can work on goals for that next.

Chapter 10
Resolve Conflicts

Whatever your goals for transformation, you'll always be dealing with others who may not share them and may resist the changes you're making. Then too, you might want to transform your relationships to be healthier and more rewarding for you. Conflicts are a natural part of any relationship. If you're like many people, you might find you could use some assistance in making conflicts less emotionally intense, rarer, and more productive.

The emotional stress of being in conflict with others can take a heavy toll, even causing headaches or other stress-related physical problems. When conflicts are giving you a headache, literally or figuratively, consult your hidden wisdom to learn more and you might gain insights that would otherwise escape you.

One man did this, and what came into his awareness was a snippet of a song with lyrics about being a man. He took a walk afterward to meditate on why that song's lyrics had come into his awareness. After all, he hadn't heard the song for years.

As a result of meditating, he realized he had received the message to *Be a man! Be tough! Don't back down!* repeatedly as a child and young man and, unconsciously, had internalized it. The song's lyrics reminded him of this experience.

Now conscious of the old message, he wanted to replace it with a healthier one that would support him in better controlling his temper during conflicts. He hoped changing his deeply held beliefs about what is manly would help him have fewer arguments and more discussions with others that were productive and respectful.

The man decided to write a new story: *While I don't seek conflicts, I don't avoid them either, because conflicts can lead to creativity and closeness instead of headaches.* It took listening to wisdom from his unconscious to recognize the message he had received as a child that was influencing him as an adult facing conflicts in relationships. Now that he was aware of it, he was consciously choosing to reject it.

What old stories about conflict are hidden inside you that need to be brought to light and rewritten? A story like *I have to win arguments* or *Admitting I might be wrong is a sign of weakness* may be getting in the way of something more valuable to you than being right or seen as strong. Maybe a story like these is preventing you from having more harmonious relationships. Your unconscious may be able to offer you insights into why you have such a strong need to see conflicts as battles between opponents—one who will win and one who will lose.

Consider using one of this book's hidden-wisdom techniques to learn more about how you experience and deal with conflicts. If you do so, you can record your experience here.

As a result of using a hidden-wisdom technique, I learned the following about how I experience and deal with conflicts and why: _____

_____

_____

_____

_____

_____

The emotional stress of being in conflict with others can take a heavy toll, even causing headaches or other stress-related physical problems.

Conflict Resolution Using the Martial Arts Wisdom of Kime and Maai

Two principles from the martial arts, *kime* and *maai*, can help us deal with conflict and avoid feeling that life is an exhausting battle. Conflict doesn't have to define our relationships with other people who are difficult, contentious, or determined to conquer or dominate us. Life is too short to let tense situations and other people's aggressive or thoughtless behavior cause us to feel angry and hurt.

Kime (key-may) means focus: the right force, at the right place, at the right time. It involves being *loose, loose, tight, loose*—remaining loose except in those moments when you need to put forth a concentrated effort. In karate or judo, kime is the moment of a focused kick, punch, strike, or throw. In a conversation with someone who is being too forceful, kime is the moment in which we set a firm boundary, speak our truth, or take some other action rooted in clarity and purpose.

When dealing with a challenging person, it's best to remain loose and listen. We need to consider their perspective and personal experiences while we remain relaxed and attentive while observing them. We benefit from asking ourselves, *What is this person's body language conveying?*

Body language can be a gesture or posture, a quality of voice, or a facial expression. Making or not making eye contact and standing close to someone rather than far away or vice versa are forms of body language, too.

If we start becoming irritated or frustrated during a conflict, we can breathe deeply, allowing our nervous system to be on alert but not hijacked by an intense fight-or-flight response that can overwhelm us with anger. Should our muscles tense up, we can consciously relax them. The goal is to have clarity and energy available to us when we recognize that it's time for us to speak. Remaining loose lets us move smoothly and quickly when we assert ourselves. In contrast, remaining tight, with our muscles tense, while waiting for our chance to win by taking a strong action will tire us out. It's best to not lose our cool as we wait for the right time to speak, trusting that we will find the right words to use.

Of course, we don't want to miss our chance to make our point. We have to be sure not to remain loose for so long that we passively retreat or give in without speaking up or taking needed action. Otherwise, we might find that often, difficult people will take advantage of us.

Maai (mah-ah-ee) is a strong partner for kime when it comes to martial arts wisdom, and we can use it in our everyday lives. **Maai is the principle of right distance: not too close, not too far.** If a competitor is too close to someone with whom they are sparring in a karate or judo match, their action will be restricted and won't have full impact. If the competitor is too far away, they won't be able to reach their opponent to make a strong impact on them. Similarly, if we're too close to or too far from a situation emotionally, it can cause problems.

Let's say that a person is attached to having a particular family member speak to them respectfully but feels that this relative habitually disrespects him. If this individual doesn't practice maai, his emotions might get the better of him. He might lose objectivity and struggle in vain to deal with the situation effectively when his relative begins raising her voice. Being too close to the situation emotionally and becoming angry can make it hard to think clearly or come up with a win-win solution. And what if the relative meant no disrespect? He has become emotionally reactive even though his relative is raising her voice for reasons that have nothing to do with him.

Now, if we're too far away from our emotions and another person's, we're also not practicing maai. Then we can lose our ability to be empathetic toward that other person when they are upset. We might too quickly dismiss their feelings and desires, thinking only of ourselves and our need for quiet and a lack of drama. When this happens, it becomes difficult to achieve a compassionate resolution to a conflict.

To have more productive conflicts, we can ask ourselves whether there are places where we are too tight—too on edge. We can try to identify situations in which we have a hard time controlling our emotions. We can think about whether we are not seeing someone's behavior clearly because we are too upset by them or too impatient.

We can also remember to be more sensitive to other people's feelings, listening attentively instead of interrupting them. Our remaining above the drama can upset them, making it hard for them to focus on finding common ground with us. Allowing them to express their emotions might not be as stressful as we might think it will be. I have discovered that sometimes, people just want to be heard and listened to long enough to feel that they are valued. Then, they shift on their own. Their emotional intensity gives way to a calmer state in which they are open to solving problems and listening to others speak. Conflicts with them can become less painful and more likely to have a good outcome.

Sometimes people avoid conflict altogether, figuring that that's the easiest and safest choice. However, this attitude can lead to feeling drained, powerless, and defeated.

All relationships involve clashes at times, and when you work at conflict resolution using martial arts wisdom, it can lead to greater trust, deeper emotional intimacy, and stronger partnerships. Leaning into a difficult situation and practicing kime and ma can help you to better handle disagreements with other people and develop effective solutions to problems.

You might want to think back to a conflict you had and fill in the following, as doing so could help you to better understand how to practice right focus and force and right distance.

The conflict I want to reflect on is this: _____

_____

_____

_____

_____

Practicing kime during this conflict, remaining loose and focused and asserting myself at just the right time with just the right amount of forcefulness, looked like/would have looked like this: _____

_____

_____

_____

Practicing maai during this conflict, remaining at the right emotional distance from the person with whom I was in conflict and the right emotional distance from my own feelings, looked like/would have looked like this: _____

_____

_____

_____

_____

Kime (key-may) means focus: the right force, at the right place, at the right time. Maai (mah-ah-ee) is the principle of right distance: not too close, not too far.

Use Your Words, Choose Your Words—and Pause Before Responding

At times, other people's behavior toward us can be frustrating, hurtful, or even infuriating. We teach our children to use their words instead of reacting physically, even violently, toward others who hurt them. It's a good relationship communication rule for everyone. However, as adults, we not only have to use our words but choose our words—carefully—when we're upset and experience conflict with someone. That can be difficult if there's no space in which the self who is rational and observant can notice what is happening and consciously choose a desired reaction.

If you can learn to create a momentary pause before you respond verbally to a situation, you're likely to find that your word choices support healthy and helpful communication more than they would otherwise. You can create this pause by training your brain over time using meditation, which will allow you to slow your emotional reactions and experience them as less intense. Then, the self who can stand back from the situation and observe what's happening will be empowered to select words that will effectively resolve the conflict, set a boundary, or both.

What should you do when someone is saying something hurtful, disrespectful, or cruel? You might want to look back at a situation where your response to someone's hurtful behavior made you feel good about yourself and your choice about which words to use during a conflict and fill in the following.

Here is an example of a time when someone said something hurtful, disrespectful, or cruel to me and I responded in a way that gives me satisfaction and even pride: _____
_____
_____

The words I chose to say were: _____
_____
_____

The response I got was: _____
_____
_____
_____

As a result, I felt: _____

_____

_____

Here is a description of a time when someone said something hurtful, disrespectful, or cruel to me and I wish I had responded differently, in a way that would have made me feel satisfied and even proud: _____

_____

_____

_____

_____

_____

_____

_____

_____

_____

Maybe at some point, you responded to an unnerving confrontation by walking away from it rather than speaking up. If so, you might want to fill in the following.

Here is an example of when I walked away from a confrontation rather than speak up, and how I felt about that choice afterward: _____

_____

_____

This is how the other person responded to my walking away: _____

_____

_____

_____

How I felt (dissatisfied, frustrated, confused, etc.) after walking away and getting the response I did: _____

_____

_____

_____

If there's something I could have done differently that would have allowed me to feel better about the confrontation ended, it's this: _____

_____

_____

_____

_____

Postponing a confrontational conversation to another time, when the other person is less angry or upset, can be a good choice. However, many people make that decision but never follow through and remind the other person of the unresolved conflict so it can be worked out. Has that ever been true for you? If so, you might want to fill in the following.

An example of my postponing a confrontational conversation to another time, but not resolving the conflict at a later point, was: _____

_____

_____

_____

_____

If I didn't try to resolve the conflict, the reason was: _____

_____

_____

_____

_____

If I came back to the conversation to resolve the conflict, these were the words I used: _____

_____

_____

_____

_____

These words helped me stand up for myself, speak my truth, and resolve the conflict without me or the other person losing control or hurting each other. Circle one: Yes No

My thoughts on whether my words were effective for resolving the conflict in a satisfactory way are: _____

_____

_____

_____

Note that you might have chosen not to resolve the conflict because you feared that you wouldn't find the right words to both express yourself and alleviate any tension between you and the other person, or you feared that you would lose your temper or that the other person would lose theirs. Sometimes, people will respond to conflict by choosing words to placate the other person, hoping to calm them down, but they end up swallowing the words they want to say that express how they're feeling and what their needs are. Not speaking up for yourself contributes to a relationship that has less emotional intimacy and trust. Then again, it can be difficult to voice your truth when you don't trust the other person to accept what you say. In my work as an analyst, I observed that often, people would say to someone, *Please—tell me how you really feel* but then react badly when they received an honest response!

Think about experimenting with different responses the next time you're in a conflict with someone. For example, when you feel criticized, you might fall into a familiar habitual response and be unaware of your other options. Some responses aren't the best choices: You can criticize the other person in return, try to convince the other person that the criticism is invalid and unfair, or say nothing, feel hurt, and quickly end the conversation, never to return to it. You could crack a self-effacing joke, but what would that accomplish besides making you feel less tense? You could respond passive aggressively, criticizing them in such a way that it's hard for them to know whether you're serious or joking but hurting their feelings nonetheless. I wouldn't recommend that.

You could also say, *Hmm, I'll have to think about that.* Keep in mind that the options for response that make you feel powerful in the moment might not be the ones that make you feel powerful—and good about yourself—later.

While it may not feel natural at first, you might want to respond to conflict with a simple statement about what you're experiencing, such as, *When you tell me I don't have a clue, I feel angry and hurt. Is that your intention?* Or you could say, *I feel devalued when you instantly dismiss my idea* and see what the other person says.

Even if you feel they are deliberately trying to provoke you, consider offering them the benefit of the doubt. You might see them back down, apologize, or make excuses for their behavior. If they continue to berate you or disrespect you, you can choose to set a boundary and state what you're doing. *I'm not having this conversation when you're yelling at me* or *I'll finish this conversation with you later when we can have it without you calling me names* are statements that set good boundaries with others.

Consider looking back at a choice you made in the past regarding how to respond to a conflict and then filling in the following.

These are my responses to conflicts that have made me feel strong in the moment, but after the conflictual conversation ended, I didn't feel strong and proud: _____

_____

_____

_____

These are my responses to conflict I've had that made me feel strong and proud both during the conflict and afterward: _____

_____

_____

_____

These are responses to conflict I would like to have in the future—because if I did, I believe I would feel strong and proud during the conflict and afterward: _____

_____

_____

_____

_____

As you become more conscious of your reactions to people who upset you, you'll find it easier to react to conflicts by making conscious choices that you feel good about—including choices about what to say. These may be different choices from what you're used to, and they may feel unnatural at first. However, if you sit with them afterward and get in touch with your thoughts and feelings, you might decide you'll stick with those choices even if you suspect they'll continue to feel awkward and unfamiliar for a while.

Not speaking up for yourself contributes to a relationship that has less emotional intimacy and trust.

Use your words—and choose them wisely—so you can achieve your goals in relationships with others and support your best possible psychological well-being.

To become better at choosing the right words and practicing kime and maai, you might want to use a hidden-wisdom technique to gain insights and energies for transformation. For example, you might dialogue with your wise inner self, your fear of conflict, or perhaps the part of yourself that either avoids conflicts or becomes too aggressive when in a conflict. Alternatively, you might want to do a journey or make a nature painting to learn more about how you deal with conflict and how to respond differently so you'll be more satisfied with the outcome.

In using a hidden-wisdom technique to learn more about how I can better manage conflicts with people, I experienced and learned the following: _____

_____

_____

_____

_____

_____

You might want to set a goal for handling conflicts based on what you learned and what you experienced energetically. Maybe there is a conflict in your life now that you would like to resolve? You can set a goal around that. If you would like to transform a habit around conflicts in general, you might want to set a goal for that. Of course, you can't necessarily predict when you'll experience a conflict again, but you can schedule check-in points when you can reflect on whether you had a conflict and if you achieved your goal for changing how you handled it.

🎯 **Keeping in mind accountability, my specific, achievable goal for making a change regarding conflict with others, which I aim to meet the next time I'm involved in a conflict, is:**

_____

_____

_____

✔️ **I achieved my goal:** Yes No (Circle one)

Any notes on what helped or hindered me in trying to reach my goal: _____

_____

_____

Chapter 11
Create the Life You Desire

"Imagination is more important than knowledge."

—Albert Einstein

Say the word *genius* and for many, Albert Einstein comes to mind. Yet for all his intellect, knowledge, and wisdom about the nature of the cosmos, Einstein valued imagination more than knowledge. Whatever you wish to create for yourself, if you begin with your imagination, you might find you dream more ambitiously than you would have if you'd only been imagining what is most likely to be possible for you. Creativity and imagination are essential for resilience—for adapting to the suddenlies (the unexpected events) of life and for writing and bringing to life a new and better story for yourself. In this chapter, you will begin to imagine what you can create for yourself and how you might transform your life and your story.

Access Your Creativity, Vitality, and Sense of Adventure

Maybe you have become caught in an old story that is no longer serving you. You might be repeating the same old patterns but yearn to feel more enlivened and live less robotically, with a greater sense of adventure and creativity. Or maybe your life seems to be going along well enough, so you don't like to complain, but part of you longs for something more.

When I was around forty years old, I felt restless, as if something were missing from my life. I didn't know what was wrong or what I wanted to experience. I felt I had fallen out of touch with my mythopoetic self, which had adventurously hitchhiked across the U.S. in my younger years, memorized poetry, written essays, and sung in a vocal group. I had experienced many successes on the practical path I had chosen. I had a good, solid career. I'd married and had kids, and I was a good provider for my family, who seemed to be happy. Yet I wanted more.

After talking with a family friend, I got the idea to study to become a Jungian analyst. My professional and personal obligations limited me to pursuing my dream part-time, but I was excited about the opportunity to let go of the sense of constriction that had been plaguing me. As

I began to take classes and undergo Jungian analysis, I felt connected to my goal and motivated to continue, even when the work was difficult. The part of me that is logical and understands numbers and business strategies and models was being expressed in my business life, but now the part of me that was fascinated by the big questions in life and by the complexity of how people behave was coming alive again.

Had I not been open to exploring something new, I might not have made that initial phone call to learn about what I would need to do become an analyst. Alternatively, I might have made it but been overwhelmed by what was involved (maybe it's good that I didn't truly take in how many years of study I'd have to commit to). Creativity means being open to new ideas and trying out new activities, approaches, and perspectives. A sense of adventurousness can help you explore possibilities that you hadn't thought about previously.

Creativity means being open to new ideas and trying out new activities, approaches, and perspectives.

If you're not sure what you would like to experience, it may be that for too long, you've been cut off from your creativity and imagination. Maybe you've told yourself it's impractical to dream about living a different kind of life, which I did for a long time. But maybe it's not as impractical as you think. Perhaps you could start making your way toward a path that you find more fulfilling, one that's more pleasing to you and Spirit. By getting in touch with your creativity, you'll start to come up with ideas about how to make your life more fulfilling and satisfying. Then, you can start identifying some goals and ways to begin trying to reach them.

Creativity and imagination don't have to be restricted to the fine arts. You don't have to be a painter or a writer to express your creativity. However, if you're like many people, you may have shut it down as you became a teenager or an adult so that you could remain focused on what you thought were more serious pursuits that would lead to a sense of security. You might find the following strategies helpful for sparking ideas and breaking out of any constrictive boxes you feel you're in.

Express Yourself through the Arts, without Judgment

You might want to engage in some sort of artistic activity with no goal in mind and not judging yourself about your talent or the results. Remember that you are doing this as an exercise to see how it feels to be creative and see what emerges, not to impress anyone. Write a poem or song, paint a picture, make a collage, or use some modeling clay to create a sculpture. Dance and see what choreography you naturally create as you move in time to the music.

Focus on how it feels to express yourself creatively. If you feel uneasy with being in touch with your creativity, explore why that is. If it's difficult for you to simply enjoy the process of creating without becoming pessimistic or criticizing yourself, free yourself by identifying what you're afraid of and why. You can do this by accessing your hidden wisdom, perhaps dialoguing with the energy of creativity or with your need to criticize and judge yourself. Remember, creativity can help you break through any obstacles or feelings of being stuck, helping you to achieve your goals.

Some things I could do to express my creativity without judging myself: _____
_____
_____
_____

Now that I expressed my creativity in a low-stakes way, here is how it felt to do that: _____
_____
_____
_____
_____

Try Doing Everyday Activities Differently

Small acts toward operating differently, which break you out of a habitual, robotic way of being, can trigger your creativity and get you thinking about what else you might want to try and how it feels to break up your routine. If you typically take a walk in the evening, you can choose a different route or go biking instead. If you usually drink wine with dinner to relax, you can do a guided visualization or journey instead and see how that feels. You might visit a place you've never been to before, such as an international grocery store or an unfamiliar restaurant, and try something new. You could take a new route to work or a friend's house or brush your teeth or write or draw with your nondominant hand. Breaking out of your rut can awaken your enthusiasm for making a big change one small decision at a time.

Some ways I could break up my routine: _____
_____
_____
_____
_____

Aim to Expand Your Life

We all have constraints. Not all medical conditions are reversible. Not all relationships can be rekindled. Not all situations can be improved, even with a great deal of time and effort on our part. However, you may be able to accept the boundaries of the box you're in if you can enrich the box's contents, learn to move more freely within it, and even expand the boundaries of the box.

A doctor friend of mine found herself increasingly agitated with the endless paperwork, long hours, and economics of practicing general medicine today. While she liked working with patients, she was feeling burned out and trapped. She saw no reasonable alternative by which she could switch her profession and replace her income. She felt as if she were in a box that was stifling her and she was fighting to escape.

My friend chose not to break out of the box and radically change her profession, finances, and lifestyle. By exploring what she most valued and becoming more aware of the positive aspects of her situation, she was able to accept her box's boundaries. Then, she experienced an internal shift: She realized how much she felt called to be a healer and what she could do to recapture the art of healing. She had been using techniques such as journeying on her own for self-exploration, but now she signed up to teach a workshop on how to use journeying for healing. She also became more appreciative of what her income and career can afford her instead of just focusing on the details of her life that bother her. She is transforming her way of thinking about being trapped in a box and expanding the walls to suit herself better.

The process of changing your story tends to be more successful and long-lasting when you first take the time to truly appreciate and honor what is working for you. Then, instead of seeing yourself as closed in by the walls of a box, you can see more possibilities and begin to write a new story for yourself despite any limitations you have come to accept.

Instead of seeing yourself as closed in by the walls of a box, you can see more possibilities and begin to write a new story for yourself despite any limitations you have come to accept.

If you feel constricted, as if you're living in a box, you are probably not going to completely change your career or lifestyle with one or two small choices that take you out of your habitual way of operating. However, ultimately, small choices do add up to larger ones. Connecting with how it feels to be creative and adventurous can renew your sense of vitality and open you up to even more ideas about what you might do differently or try for the first time. Give yourself credit for small changes you make. Feel proud of these. Then, you might find that you're ready to tackle more changes. One creative change often gives birth to others.

A way in which I feel constricted or boxed in is: _____

_____

_____

One thing I could do to feel less constricted and expand the box is: _____

_____

_____

One thing I could do right now to expand my life and renew my sense of creativity and adventurousness despite my restrictions is: _____

_____

_____

_____

Let Vitality Cross Over from One Chapter of Your Life to Another

You might want to look at various chapters in your life—your health, relationships, psychology (thoughts and feelings), job/career/vocation, relationship to God or Spirit, way of being of service in the world, and so on—and note where you feel most or least enlivened. Maybe you lack vitality in all these areas or in some more than others. Think about if you can bring some of the vitality and sense of curiosity and enthusiasm from one area of your life into another.

Do some exploring: Try some new activities in one chapter of your life and see whether it affects another. If you engage in a new spiritual practice, such as walking a labyrinth or taking a journey facilitated by recordings of drumming, rattling, or hypnotic music to help you shift your awareness, it might open your eyes to how you could infuse your job or career with a fresh approach. Cooking a new dish might turn on the faucet of your creativity and adventurousness just enough to get you thinking about how you would like to be more creative in how you give in service to others. Maybe you'll volunteer at a soup kitchen or work in a community garden that offers free vegetables, fruits, and herbs to low-income people. Changes in one chapter of your life often lead to changes in another.

If there's a chapter in my life where I feel enlivened, it is: _____

_____

Drawing on what I know about what makes me feel enlivened, an idea about how I could bring more vitality into a chapter of my life is: _____

_____

_____

🎯 Keeping in mind the need for accountability, I'm setting this specific, achievable goal for bringing vitality into at least one chapter of my life: _____

_____

_____

_____

_____

✓ **I achieved my goal:** Yes No (Circle one)

Any notes on what helped or hindered me in trying to reach my goal: _____

_____

_____

_____

Changes in one chapter of your life often lead to changes in another.

Allow Yourself to Be a Little Uncomfortable as You Make Changes

The changes you make as you try to be more creative don't have to be major, but you might want to choose ones that will make you feel at least a little awkward or uncomfortable. Getting out of your comfort zone can help you feel more adventurous and creative overall as you experience that you can do something different despite your uneasiness—and enjoy the activity.

Something I could do that would take me a little out of my comfort zone: _____

_____

_____

_____

🎯 Keeping in mind the need for accountability, I'm setting this specific, achievable goal for getting a little out of my comfort zone: _____

_____

_____

_____

✓ **I achieved my goal:** Yes No (Circle one)

Any notes on what helped or hindered me in trying to reach my goal: _____

_____

_____

_____

In Your Imagination, Visit the Past and the Future

Letting your mind wander to the past and future can help you reach your goals and experience self-understanding, self-acceptance, and self-love. All of these can help you claim your creativity and begin to fashion the life you desire instead of living robotically and feeling unfulfilled.

It's true that reminiscing about the past, pining for the days when you were younger and more fit, accomplished, admired, or respected might make you melancholy, especially if you have regrets. Maybe listening to the music you listened to when you were younger provides you bittersweet pleasure as you think about the joy you had and that may never come again. However, memories can remind you of your ability to engage the world with a sense of enthusiasm, ready to create something new. Remembering who you once were might help you reclaim lost optimism and forgotten courage that can serve you today and into the future.

You can experience recapturing aspects of your past self by using the following hidden-wisdom technique.

Hidden-Wisdom Technique: Visualization to Observe Yourself in the Past

Find a place where you feel comfortable sitting, settle in, close your eyes, and focus on your breath or a mantra until you feel relaxed and focused. Then, in your mind's eye, stand next to the self you once were, sharing each other's energy, emotions, and wisdom. Imagine you are soaking in the excitement you had in the past while keeping your wisdom gained through experience. Visualize your past self sharing with you positive, helpful emotions or perspectives that you lost or left behind. Notice what you feel and see.

And notice your current-day self's response. For example, does it want to put down your younger self for having certain qualities, like being optimistic and trusting rather than jaded and skeptical?

After you've done this visualization, you can write down what you felt as you connected with the younger you. Pay attention to whether you reclaimed some of what you once had or rejected those qualities.

Notes on my exercise imagining myself soaking in my younger self's energy, emotions, and wisdom: _____

_____

_____

_____

_____

_____

_____

_____

You can't change the past, but you can alter how you feel about it and how it affects you today. While you might think your younger self was foolhardy, doing a visualization to connect with the energy of that self might help you reclaim your adventurousness that was related to behavior you now see as foolhardy. You might then look at who you once were with more compassion—and even perhaps with some pride as you recognize you had some terrific qualities. Yes, you might want to temper them now that you have more wisdom and life experience. But reclaiming your adventurousness or some other quality might help you write and bring to life a new and better story.

And be open to the possibility that where you are in your life presently is better in many ways than where you were in the past. Are you grateful for the story you've created so far?

Next, imagine traveling into the future so you can daydream about the possibilities you would like to make your reality.

Hidden-Wisdom Technique: Visualization of a Future Day

Imagine yourself waking up and about to experience a perfect day in the future. Where are you? What are you going to do before breakfast? What are you going to eat, and what are you going to do after you've finished your meal? Imagine the sensations you feel as you go about each activity on this perfect day. Pay attention to the emotions you feel as the day unfolds and as you engage in each desired activity.

Perhaps when you think about or imagine what lies ahead you become anxious. Maybe you worry about what you might lose or how you might suffer instead of becoming excited about opportunities for joy, growth, and new experiences appearing. If any feelings of constriction, impatience, or hesitancy arise while doing this visualization, pay attention to them. Allow yourself to feel them and see if that makes them shift. If they don't change, you can end the visualization and do a dialogue with the emotion you felt or with your wise inner self to learn more. Then, try this exercise again to see if you have a different emotional experience.

If your imagining the future doesn't cause any constriction, impatience, or hesitancy to arise, continue to experience in your mind a perfect day. Afterward, let yourself feel the satisfaction of having experienced everything you wished to have experienced—and consider recording your experience below.

Reflections on my visualization of the future and my perfect day: _____
_____
_____
_____
_____
_____
_____

Imagine possibilities you would like to make your reality.

Many people are told not to daydream—to be realistic instead. However, if you want to make positive changes in your life, it's good to ponder possibilities. You might want to imagine the future and what you might experience in any specific chapter of your life. If you choose to do so, write your notes about it here.

I learned and experienced the following because I imagined a future in which I experienced better things in a chapter of my life: _____
_____
_____
_____
_____
_____
_____

129

Our imaginings can help us bring into being what otherwise might not materialize.

In my quest to become better at working with people as a psychologist and helping them write better stories for their lives, I have studied with many shamans (indigenous healers). I've learned that they will often shift their consciousness so they can track the future of the person who has come to them seeking healing. In other words, they do what we would call using their intuition to see where the person could be headed. Shamans might see the most likely trajectory of that person's path, but they look for a preferred one. Knowing what could become the person's experience in the future if no changes are made, the shaman brings back helpful energies so the seeker's energy field can be altered, sending them on a path to a more desired future. I believe that visualizations in which you imagine what might happen in a better future can help you experience that future even if it seems an unlikely one.

A friend of mine told me the story of someone she met who said that as an eight-year-old child growing up in a rural area, she had written a list of five things she absolutely wanted to do when she grew up. Number one on that list was *Work for the Metropolitan Opera in New York City*. Believe it or not, when my friend met this woman years later, the woman was doing just that! Setting an intention can be extremely powerful—if you follow through with actions to turn that dream into your reality.

One benefit to imagining different scenarios is that you can recognize and honor your desire to change your life for the better even though you have much to be thankful for today. You can retain all that you are grateful for right now in this moment yet experience even greater happiness, health, and abundance.

So, don't be too hard on yourself if you find your mind wandering to the past as a feeling of nostalgia arises—or wandering to the future as you daydream about achieving what you desire. Be present in the moment when you can, but use your nostalgic reminiscing and your daydreaming as inspiration. Commit to working with the past and the future through daydreaming, envisioning, and remembering in addition to being present in what's happening today. Releasing what is not working for you, bringing in what you desire, and changing the path you are on may be more possible than you think.

Begin to Design a New Future for Yourself

In the physical world, things have a past and a future, a beginning, and an end. For example, I'm sitting on a chair in my office at my desk that I've had for more than fifty years. At some point, this chair was just an idea in someone's head. They designed it and then, it was engineered and constructed from materials like wood, fabric, and metal. I don't know how long its natural life will be. It squeaks when I lean back, which I could probably fix. At some point, whatever repairs I make to the chair won't be enough to make it comfortable, and it will reach the end of its natural life. Then what? Will it be tossed in a landfill? Recycled or repurposed? I don't know, but I do know this: Everything, including people, has a beginning and end, a useable lifespan that varies. Who we are is influenced by our parents' DNA, our upbringing, our life choices, and our environment. You have a certain number of years you will live. If you want to feel happy and fulfilled, you might want to make more conscious choices about what to experience.

If you want to design a new future for yourself, why not start today? Think of at least three ways to make more time for doing things that support your health and happiness—such as exercise and spending more time having fun—and three ways to spend less time doing things you don't have to do and that you don't value. Maybe you want to travel to a particular place, complete a project such as writing a memoir, or mentor someone. Maybe you want to spend less time doing unnecessary chores, watching television, and engaging with social media. You don't have to come up with specific goals just yet—that comes next.

Three things I want to make more time for to secure a healthier, happier future: _____

_____

_____

_____

Three things I want to devote less time to so I have more time for more desired activities:

_____

_____

_____

Now come up with specific goals for making time for what you value and spending less time on what you don't.

🎯 **Keeping in mind the need for accountability, I'm setting these three specific, achievable goals for making time for what I value and spending less time on what I don't:**

1. _____

_____

_____

2. _____

_____

_____

3. _____

_____

_____

✔ **I achieved my goals:** Yes No (Circle one)

Any notes on what helped or hindered me in trying to reach my goals: _____

_____

_____

_____

Find Resources for Change

Sometimes what you need for bringing about a much-desired change is resources of time, energy, and money. Are you sure that you have exhausted every possible avenue in researching what resources are available to you? Think of a way you might bring in greater resources to allow you to more easily do what you find valuable and spend less time on activities you don't value.

I could bring in resources for more of what I want to do and less of what I don't want to do by: _____

_____

_____

Often what you need is creativity and flexibility. Maybe the time has passed for you to achieve your goal in the form you imagined, but perhaps there's another way to reach it. For example, you might not own a lake house despite years of yearning for one, but maybe you can spend more time in lake houses enjoying them without owning, using your resources wisely to figure out ways to make that happen. Creativity and flexibility can help you find ways to change your story that you hadn't thought of before. If you had trouble identifying resources you could bring in, look at that question again and allow yourself to be creative and flexible. Is it easier to answer the question now?

Often, what you need to find resources for change is creativity and flexibility.

You don't have to wait for your chair to start squeaking or for health challenges related to aging to awaken you to your potential for living a more fulfilling life and using your time more consciously, in ways that give you greater satisfaction.

Let your imagination run free. Consult your hidden wisdom to gain ideas on what you can let go of or bring into your life to recharge your creativity. If you get some ideas for goals that you haven't yet recorded in this book, write them into the appendix and mark on your calendar the dates on which you are going to check in with yourself to be sure you hold yourself accountable for meeting your aims.

In the next chapter, I'll teach you practical ways to maximize your chances of success at achieving your goals and find guidance on whether to change your goals or recommit to them.

Chapter 12
Resilience When Presented with Life's Suddenlies

I have often led workshops for people who want to learn techniques for gaining insights and momentum that will help them transform their lives in some way. At the end of our work together, I will typically ask everyone to gather around in a circle as I start a story I want them to add to. I begin by saying, "Once upon a time, a group of people came together …" Then I pass to the person on my left the rattle I'm holding—a shamanic tool I use to help them get into a more relaxed state of mind than they would be otherwise. I ask them to add to the story before passing the rattle onto the next person in our circle, who should then continue the story.

The rattle and the story make their way around the circle, with each participant adding something. When the rattle makes its way back to me, instead of saying something like, *And so it was*, or *And this concludes the workshop*, or even, *And they all lived happily ever after*, I say, "And then suddenly …"

That startles them. I explain that I've done this because regardless of how much we plan, analyze, and take action to make our stories about what we want to happen come to life, there will always be unexpected "suddenlies." These are the plot twists in our stories that swiftly and dramatically change the road we are on. *And they offer opportunities.*

You, like many people, may have suddenly faced changes you never anticipated. You didn't ask to have your life disrupted, to have your movements restricted and choices you took for granted suddenly gone, but here you are. Now what?

It's your turn to decide what your story will be now. How will you respond to this new moment?

You might begin to worry about the future, anticipating all that might happen tomorrow and in the weeks and months to come. You might distract yourself with entertainment. You might get stuck in anger over how you didn't get to reach your goals due to circumstances beyond your control. And you might work with this chapter because the advice and strategies you'll find in here may help you resolve any inner conflicts you're having about persevering versus giving up.

135

Use a Setback as an Opportunity to Learn Something New

As you deal with a "suddenly" that has disrupted your life, you can take the opportunity to think about what you have yet to learn and master. Maybe you always wanted to learn how to better manage anxiety, be more organized, or something else. Maybe the suddenly you experienced, which looks like a setback, is offering you an opportunity to learn something new.

Life has rhythms. As a businessman, I've enjoyed successes when I reaped the harvest of hard work. I have also had to cut back my operations here and there due to downturns. I had to plan something new. Fear that I didn't know what to do, that I might make a mistake, tempted me to pine for the good times that had passed and regret that they did not last longer, but I knew I had to look forward. A harvest would come again. Paradoxically, being forced to do things with fewer people and resources often led me to find new ways of operating. Those changes, in turn, led to even more efficient and effective methods for getting things done.

I've learned that sometimes, instead of resisting a downturn in a cycle, it's best to accept it and explore its possibilities. Unseen options may be available. When you feel blocked and unable to move forward, and none of your efforts seem to be paying off, trying harder to force a situation to change may not be the best choice. A downturn in a cycle of business or life offers a chance to observe, assess, ponder, plan, and plant so we can enjoy a new harvest. You might want to reframe the downturn as a time to imagine what else you might create and learn.

As you think about your suddenly, consider filling in the following.

An example of a suddenly (unexpected turn of events) that felt like a setback but presented me with an opportunity: _____

_____

_____

_____

_____

_____

If you have trouble answering the question, you can try a dialogue with the suddenly that threw you off course or with your wise inner self or your creativity. If you do this, record here what you learned.

After a dialogue to learn more about the opportunity the suddenly I experienced presents, these are my thoughts: _____

_____

_____

_____

_____

_____

Suddenlies—the plot twists in our stories—offer opportunities.

Address Any Sense of Tiredness or Lethargy

One of the most common complaints people share with physicians and therapists is that they feel tired and run down. It can be very frustrating when you feel too fatigued to take part in enjoyable activities and you're less productive than you would like. Setting and working toward goals can be difficult if you're feeling exhausted.

Maybe you feel sad, angry, or guilty and ashamed because you can't do more. These challenging emotions and thoughts can make you feel stressed, which in turn may exacerbate your sense of tiredness. You might be wondering, *Why am I so tired, and what can I do about it?* If so, both your conscious and unconscious mind can help you.

Think about the foods you are eating. Are they mostly plant-based, whole foods such as vegetables, fruits, and legumes, which have plenty of fiber and support health and stamina? This type of diet can help you avoid the spikes and dips in blood sugar levels that you'll experience if your diet includes a lot of highly processed foods, particularly sugars. If you're often tired or fatigued, you might want to work with a physician and a nutritionist to improve your diet so you can enjoy more energy.

Even if you're sleeping for at least eight hours, quality of sleep matters. If you snore or wake often or both, if you don't dream, or if you wake up feeling tired instead of refreshed, you might want to consult a doctor for help with improving your sleep. While it isn't possible for everyone, try to get at least eight full hours of sleep every night. Go to sleep at the same time every night. Don't drink alcohol or caffeine later in the day if it interferes with your sleep. Avoid drinking too many liquids at night. Make sure your bedroom is cool and dark at night, and don't use it to do work—keep laptops and cell phones in other rooms. Have a bedtime routine that will relax you, but avoid screentime for at least an hour before you go to bed. All these habits are known to improve the quality of sleep.

You might want to reflect on your lifestyle choices and set a goal to make changes that will help you to be less tired.

🎯 **Keeping in mind the need for accountability, I'm setting this specific, achievable goal for becoming less tired:** _____

_____

_____

✓ **I achieved my goal:** Yes No (Circle one)

Any notes on what helped or hindered me in trying to reach my goal: _____

_____

_____

While your tiredness might seem purely physical, it may have psychological causes. Once when on a shamanic journey, I encountered Harlequin-like figures who weren't friendly. I paid attention to my emotional response to them. After the journey, I realized they represented a robotic approach to life I needed to let go of. Maybe you, too, need to let go of a mechanistic, and robotic approach to your life or some aspect of it?

Getting done what needs to be done can bury those parts of ourselves that long for a sense of meaning and purpose. Some people wake up one day and realize that they've been trying to nourish themselves with activities that make a difference in the world but haven't been able to do so for whatever reason. As a result, they're going through the motions of life in a robotic, deadening way. Maybe you need to breathe vitality back into your life with some new activity or habit that would enliven you. Laughing more, dancing more, being more playful, becoming a better listener, and reaching out to people who could use mentoring are all ways to live life with more purpose, meaning, and greater liveliness.

Then too, consider the sources of any stress you're having that could be zapping your energy because of their psychological toll. Reading the news can be stressful—so can relationships, even if you care deeply about the other person. You might need more alone time. And if you find it energizing to socialize, you might want to be more discerning about the people you are socializing with. Are they people who help you feel revitalized or people who frustrate and upset you, making you feel drained? You might want to start thinking about ways you can limit stressors—and set a specific goal around reducing stress.

◎ **Keeping in mind the need for accountability, I'm setting this specific, achievable goal for reducing one specific source of stress:** _____

_____

_____

_____

✔ **I achieved my goal:** Yes No (Circle one)

Any notes on what helped or hindered me in trying to reach my goal: _____

_____

_____

_____

You might think, *I know why I am so tired, but I can't do anything more about it!* Your hidden wisdom might be able to help you find the root cause and learn to live with your tiredness and work around it. For example, if you experience fatigue because of a health condition that you're striving to address, you might need to reduce your expectations of how much you can accomplish.

Consider using the following hidden-wisdom technique to cue your unconscious to bring into your conscious mind valuable insights about the roots of your lack of energy.

Hidden-Wisdom Technique: Receiving Wisdom with Help from the Earth

To start, lie on the floor or better yet, lie on the earth in a natural area, connecting with the earth's energy, as it can affect your own energy field.

When you are settled on the floor or the ground, breathe mindfully, focusing on the sensation and rhythm of your breath. As you draw your attention to your breathing, begin to observe the feeling of your body against the floor, grass, or sand below your body. Keep drawing your attention back to your breathing again every time your mind begins to wander. When you're relaxed and you feel an energetic shift has happened, silently dialogue with the earth, asking it about your tiredness. One who did so saw a pile of white pouring through a doorway, almost as if a snowdrift had come into a room when someone opened the door. She came to realize she had let too much sugar slip into her diet and needed to close the door on it, so to speak.

---

* You can access a recording of this hidden-wisdom technique on YouTube at https://www.youtube.com/watch?v=XWIoSZf_7-4&t=221s

While lying down on the earth and relaxing, you might fall asleep! If so, your body is telling you that you are sleep deprived. Listen to that message and act on it. Then, try the exercise again when you are more rested.

If you dialogued with the earth or anything else to learn about your tiredness, you can record your experience here.

Notes on my dialogue about my tiredness: _____

_____

_____

_____

_____

_____

_____

_____

_____

While your tiredness might seem purely physical, it may have psychological causes.

Let Go of Any Anxiety or Pessimism

Anyone who struggles to manage anxiety can tell you that just thinking about the problem of managing it can make them more anxious—and tired! Anxiety is like a snake devouring its own tail, a loop of *what ifs* and negative thinking that can make someone feel jittery and unable to relax. Letting go of anxiety energetically can help.

Although we tend to think of anxiety as something negative, consider for a moment the benefits of feeling anxious. It can make you more alert and vigilant. Nervous drivers may check their mirrors more often or hesitate before pulling out into oncoming traffic and wait for a better opportunity to join its flow. Stress can make you perform better when doing public speaking under pressure. Perhaps you can start to work with your anxiety, learning what it has to teach you. Maybe it is telling you to pay closer attention to something. Maybe it is simply reminding you that change and uncertainty can be difficult, so be aware that you're dealing with change and don't be too hard on yourself if you're feeling worried.

Think back to the last time you were anxious and answer the following. If you have trouble figuring out what your anxiety was telling you, try dialoguing with it or some aspect of your hidden wisdom, such as your wise inner self, to learn more.

The last time I was anxious, this was happening: _____

_____

_____

_____

If my anxiety could speak, this is what it would have said to me: _____

_____

_____

_____

Now that I see what my anxiety was telling me, here's what I think about its message at that time: _____

_____

_____

_____

Once you draw your focus to what you are anxious about and you learn what you need to learn, or observe what you need to observe, the energy of your anxiety will have served its purpose. Release it so you can bring in a more positive and productive energy. Soon you might find yourself entering a state of enthusiasm, curiosity, creativity, or pleasure.

Exercise: Walk in Nature to Release Anxiety

The next time you're feeling anxious, listen to your anxiety to see what its message might be. If you're not sure, try walking in nature. After a few minutes, when you are feeling a little more relaxed, or after reaching a spot in nature you find especially soothing, stop and dialogue with nature about your anxiety or a situation that's making you anxious. If you do this exercise, you might want to record the answers you received and any experiences of a shift in your energy or mood.

What I learned about my anxiety from dialoguing with nature to learn more and release my anxiety: _____

_____

_____

Research shows that nature walks can reduce the levels of stress hormones in your blood and shift your energy, helping you feel relaxed. If you take a nature walk after setting your intention to release the energy of anxiety, pay attention to how you feel afterward. It may become easier to see how irrational your anxious thoughts can be and how they can overwhelm you when you don't use techniques for releasing the energy of anxiety.

Play with Metaphors to Help You Gain Insights about Transformation

Asking yourself direct questions about difficult changes you've had to deal with has value, but you also might want to play with metaphors. Figures of speech that aren't literal can yield insights and perhaps help you regain optimism about your power to change your life for the better. Then you can take what you've learned and consciously craft a new and better story for yourself.

For example, there's a metaphor from my own life and work that has helped me better understand myself and the changes I have gone through. Early in my business career, I took a job heading up an oil and gas company, so I've often thought about how the transformational process of turning organic matter into oil and refining it into gasoline relates to my own story of change. Oil was formed when organic matter—long-dead plants and animals—became crushed by layers upon layers of sediment and eventually turned into oil. The oil can eventually make its way up to the surface of the earth, and its seeping and eruptions help it to be spotted and accessed. Sometimes companies do seismic surveys to discover where crude oil might be located deep beneath the earth's surface. Once oil has been extracted from the earth, it can be refined through high temperatures and cooling to form gasoline and diesel oil, which can fuel engines.

Looking back on my journey from businessman to clinical psychologist to Jungian analyst and shamanic practitioner and finally, to a stage of life in which my focus is giving back in service to others, I've asked myself questions you might want to ask yourself, playing with this oil-and-gas metaphor:

Have pressure and time influenced and transformed you, and if so, how? _____
_____
_____
_____

How have you managed releases and eruptions from your past? _____
_____
_____
_____

What, if anything, has seeped through into your awareness from your unconscious, which is below the surface of your ordinary consciousness? _____
_____
_____
_____

What, if anything, did you do with what you discovered after it seeped through to your consciousness or was released or erupted? _____
_____
_____
_____

If you've discovered an energy/quality through accessing your hidden wisdom, what was it and has it been affecting you? _____
_____
_____
_____

If the energy/quality you discovered affected you negatively, how might it serve you positively?
_____
_____
_____
_____

What, if anything, used to be alive inside you but seemed to die or somehow became transformed into something else? _____
_____
_____
_____

Did something useful come about because of that alive thing dying or transforming, and if so, what came about? _____

_____

_____

What have you learned from the efforts you made and the emotions you experienced at a time when you were in transition? _____

_____

_____

_____

Too often, when change is thrust upon us or we're unhappy with our current stories and want to change them, we forget our past lessons about what we can do to manage transitions well and make positive changes stick. Maybe there's a metaphor regarding change that has always spoken to you, or maybe you want to work with one of these transformation metaphors:

- The transformation from a caterpillar into a butterfly
- The transformation from a tadpole into a frog
- The transformation of flour, water, salt, and yeast into bread

Choose one and play with it. Then fill in the following:

A metaphor about change that speaks to me is: _____

_____

_____

_____

If there are steps of transformation in this metaphor (for example, a caterpillar stops to spin a chrysalis before it can transform into a butterfly), this is what they are: _____

_____

_____

_____

How it feels to be the thing about to be transformed (for example, oil, a caterpillar, a tadpole, or the ingredients for bread—use your imagination to feel what it's like to be this thing):

_____

_____

_____

_____

Now you might want to imagine you are transitioning—you are a dying sea urchin that will someday become oil, a caterpillar turning into a butterfly, a tadpole losing its tail, or wheat being combined with other ingredients and kneaded into dough. Imagine the entire process of change with all its steps, right up until you are transformed. You can record here what you felt when imagining that you were experiencing this transition.

In imagining my transformation, the following thoughts, images, sensations, and/or emotions came to me: _____

_____

_____

_____

Here is how I would describe the transformation I experienced and the outcome: _____

_____

_____

_____

Now, if you like, think about transformations you've undergone in real life and fill in the following.

What if any connections I see between what I just experienced in my imagination and what I have experienced during real-life transformations: _____

_____

_____

_____

What playing with metaphors has taught me about myself and change: _____

_____

_____

_____

_____

What you might discover is that you want to write an optimistic story such as:

- I'm still in the dark, but the cocoon is warm and safe, and I trust in this process.
- I'm always evolving, and changes can take time. I can be patient with myself.
- I'm learning to trust that everything will be okay during and after a transition.

The more you play with a metaphor using your rational mind and your imagination, the more likely you are to gain insights that can help you with whatever changes you're facing now. Having played with metaphors to help you become optimistic about transformation, and identified any fears or worries you might have, you might now want to add some final thoughts about what you learned. You can do this in the form of a poem if you like. When I was undergoing a time of transition, I wrote free form poetry to express how I felt about change. I found doing this helped me get in touch with my feelings and be okay with any hesitance I had regarding making changes in my life. Here's one of my poems from that time:

Waves

The lake's waves roiled

blue and mud-brown intermingled

Inexorably moving into shore

and then again, again, again.

Where does the water really come from,

and whence does it return?

Does it learn from each visitation to the shore

or does it flow mindlessly?

The lake smiles at the question.

"Look at me," she says,

"I repeat my dance of life with exquisite variation.

The sun, the moon, wind, stars, and earth are my partners,

subtly moving with me,

changing and being changed."

The conductor enjoys the dance and orchestration,

never knowing for sure the actual composition.

The birds and other animals move to the music,

being fed and feeding.

Humans find their place by dancing

or are swept away by the music of life and submerged.

Fish know how to be in the water.

You might want to express your thoughts on transformation in sentences, pictures, or poetry here.

Don't Be a Perfectionist Who Is Too Hard on Yourself

Striving for excellence can lead to very satisfying achievements, but when is enough enough? Do you really need more money, praise, and attention, or a greater sense of control?

Persistence is good—except when it's not. When you're too hard on yourself, you can find that your life is not what you'd like it to be.

Perfectionism often involves losing sight of what is most important. If you can't let go of a project until you are satisfied that you've made it perfect, you may miss deadlines. You might cause others stress because they want to move on to another activity and you're preventing them because you expect them to put your need for perfectionism ahead of their needs. If your perfectionism is getting in your way, you might find you are harshly judging yourself. How important is perfection, really?

If you have a tendency toward perfectionism, you might want to fill in the following.

An example of a time when my perfectionism served me and an example of a time when it

didn't: _____

_____

_____

_____

_____

Perfectionism can be a gift that allows you to do an excellent job at something, but it can also slow you down, frustrate you and others, and cause you to miss deadlines or put too much effort into an activity when you want more time for another.

You might choose to dialogue with your perfectionism to learn more about what's stopping you from letting go of it when it's not serving you. Alternatively, you might dialogue with your resistance to doing certain things imperfectly or to delegating tasks to other people to see what you can learn. If you choose to do a dialogue, you can write about it here and perhaps set a goal to lighten up on yourself.

My experience dialoguing to learn more about my perfectionist tendencies was: _____

_____

_____

_____

_____

Keeping in mind the need for accountability, my specific, achievable goal to become less of a perfectionist is: _____

_____

_____

_____

Did you accomplish your goal, and if so, what helped? _____

_____

_____

If you didn't meet your goal, why do you think that is? _____

_____

You might want to do a ritual to let go of your perfectionistic tendencies or any other energies you want to release. Here is an energy-releasing ritual you can use that will also allow you to bring in a new energy.

Exercise: Ritual for Energy-Releasing and Energy-Absorbing

Go outdoors to a river or stream and find some leaves or twigs you can float downstream. Sit on the bank looking at the water, a stack of leaves or twigs by your side. Meditate into a state of relaxation. Then, set an intention to release any energy that is no longer serving you, such as the energy of your perfectionistic tendencies. Pick up a twig or leaf and blow into it the energy that you would like to release. Then place the twig or leaf in the water and watch it float away. Continue doing this, blowing energy into twigs and leaves and releasing them into the water, until you feel you have let go of all the energy you needed to release.

Next, pick up a twig or leaf and blow into it an energy you would like to bring into your life, such as energy that can help you be less concerned with perfection. Place the object in the water. Watch it float away. Continue doing this until you feel you have gained the energy you need. As a variation, you can do this with sticks you toss into a fire and watch burn.

Another way to address perfectionism is to be sure that if you meet a goal, however small, you take time to let yourself feel proud for having pushed yourself. When you've made one good change that stuck, it's important to reinforce that success. You'll likely find it easier to believe that this one positive change will lead to another—and to stop yourself from focusing on any changes you weren't able to make.

Self-doubt, judgment, and perfectionism can feel very constricting. The tension they cause you might be a sign that you need to shift your focus to achieve more satisfying results. Your goals might not be right for you given where you are in your life at this moment. Maybe you've outgrown a goal. Use the tools in this book for exploring your goals so you can get clear on whether you want to persevere, change your goals, or abandon them altogether.

Accept the Need to Move on from Losses

When we experience losses, we can always take some comfort in knowing that endings lead to beginnings. We lose people—and new people enter our lives. Situations end, but then new ones come into being.

Change is inevitable, but it's natural for us to struggle with it. When I was a practicing

Jungian analyst and clinical psychologist, many of my clients came to me because they were in transition and in need of guidance and support during a major life change. Even if you eagerly anticipate a transition to something better, you might feel mixed emotions because with these beginnings come endings. We must acknowledge our losses so we can move on from them and be open to what is being born or appearing on the horizon.

Moving on from losses is easier when you release the past and your emotions, clearing out the old to make way for the new. In your process of responding to losses and endings, let yourself feel any fear, anger, or sadness. In feeling and observing them, you help yourself to release their energy. Uncomfortable though it may be to cry, feel scared, or experience being angry, experiencing and releasing these emotions opens you up to an energetic shift. Then, it will be easier to bring to life a new and better story, one that replaces the old one that was focused on loss. You'll probably find it easier to feel optimistic, curious, and even excited as you transition into a new story that you have consciously chosen for yourself.

And begin to think of a new story to replace the old one. The new story can include optimistic thoughts about the future and the possibilities that lie ahead of you. For example, a story like, *I'm sad and upset about that chapter in my life having ended* can turn into *I'm sad that chapter ended, but I'm eagerly looking for opportunities to have new experiences that will bring me joy and fulfillment.* A story like, *I can't eat my favorite foods anymore, and I hate having to exercise* can be replaced with, *I choose not to eat the way I used to or live a sedentary life anymore, but I'm enjoying learning how to eat more healthfully and exercising in pleasurable ways. And as I'm learning, I'm seeing the results of making lifestyle changes.* Try it out:

My story about a loss: _____

_____

_____

_____

My new story that acknowledges the loss while I look forward to the future: _____

_____

_____

_____

Often, we have a hard time moving on from losses because we're clinging to a belief that the situation we were in—a particular job or romantic relationship, for example—was the only one that could lead to happiness. We might believe that we will never be as joyful as we once were no matter what new situation arises. You may have to bring in the confidence that you can find and create a new situation that is rewarding and enjoyable.

Often, we have a hard time moving on from losses because we're clinging to a belief that the situation we were in—a particular job or romantic relationship, for example—was the only one that could lead to happiness.

You have now taken time to imagine what you might want to create in the future, perhaps going beyond what you initially thought you should want to achieve or experience. You've worked to uncover any hidden blocks to creating the life you desire and experiencing resilience after setbacks and patience during transitions. Now it's time to focus on your relationship with your spirituality—and with nature, which can help you see your problems as less overwhelming, experience your spiritual nature, and learn valuable lessons.

Part III
Transformations Regarding Spirituality, Health, and Your Mortality

Chapter 13
Connecting with Your Spirituality and with Nature

Regardless of any religious teachings or practices you might have been exposed to, you might be like many people today who don't identify with a particular religion. A 2023 Pew Research poll showed that 28 percent of Americans identify as "none of the above" in a list of religious identities. Some of these people are atheists, but many believe in God/Spirit/Source. This chapter has ideas you can use to explore your spirituality and discover new ways to experience and express it that might fall outside the boundaries of what your religious background has taught you. You might learn that your relationship to your spiritual essence can make your problems seem less daunting.

If you have strong religious beliefs and identify with a particular religion, you might be uncomfortable with some of the questions and exercises in this chapter. Feel free to skip them and only work with any that you feel will help you write a better story about your relationship with God or Spirit. Ultimately, it is up to you to decide what hidden-wisdom work you'll do to improve any of the chapters of your life and whether it benefits you.

Your Relationship with Source and Its Benefits

Each of us can change our relationship with the loving, creative, wise consciousness known as God, Spirit, the Tao, a Higher Power—there are many names for this life force. I call it Source because I believe all love and all resources come from this divine source. If you feel disconnected from Source, you might want to work on your relationship with this loving consciousness.

If you don't believe such a thing exists, or you're uncomfortable with the concept of a powerful divine being, maybe you've had some unpleasant experiences of religion and church or with people who were religious but who harmed you in some way. Even so, you might want to explore the possibility that there is a loving, wise consciousness you can connect to. You may have been taught there are harsh punishments for not believing in God, but many who do believe in a Higher Power do not think that this loving consciousness wants to punish people who are nonbelievers. You don't have to let old stories hold you back from exploring your spirituality and potentially having a relationship with Source that could be profoundly satisfying and rewarding for you. You can choose to write a new story of this relationship.

You can start with identifying your beliefs and stories about God, religion, and spirituality. It's important to recognize these stories that your hidden wisdom is aware of so you can consciously decide whether to keep them or change them.

A better relationship with Source can provide many benefits. It might make you feel you are less alone, part of something larger than yourself, and proud to be connected to something grand and loving. This can help you experience less anxiety, greater faith in your future, and a deeper sense of purpose. And a better relationship with Source can also help relativize your problems, that is, make you feel that they aren't so big and upsetting after all because you have a new perspective on them.

Feeling a connection to Source might help you to be more generous and kinder to others, helping you to feel good about yourself. It might also make it easier for you to serve others lovingly even when the people you are assisting are unpleasant. Such service can provide a sense of meaning and purpose, which can lead to a feeling of fulfillment because you recognize that however large or small your contribution, you matter. For example, on the surface, a handyman does home repairs, yet he also removes sources of stress from people. Giving people a greater sense of peace is his larger purpose. When you connect with Source, you might also find faith that you, as one person, can truly make a meaningful difference in the world.

Other benefits to improving your relationship with Source might be feeling more gratitude and contented—and becoming more courageous, strong, and optimistic when times are difficult. With more awareness and a stronger feeling of connection to Source, you might well find that you live your life more fully instead of in a constricted way.

Also, each of us has a unique set of talents and desires. If you're constantly conforming to other people's expectations instead of listening to your heart's messages about how you want to live, reconnecting with Source might change that and help you to live more authentically, in synch with your deepest values and desires.

A good relationship with Source can make it easier to consciously decide what to devote attention to and what to get rid of because it no longer serves you. You can gain a sense of freedom to choose new possibilities for yourself and your life. You might discard identities or roles only to have them reborn within you in fresh configurations. In other words, how you parent, teach, heal, advocate—how you do anything—can transform. By disidentifying with a term like *parent* or *healer*, you can begin to explore new meanings for those terms. You can come to recognize that you don't have to be the same kind of parent, teacher, healer, or advocate that you have been. And in making decisions, you might feel you are able to be guided by a deeper wisdom than that which you have experienced before.

Finally, if you are facing your mortality, you might find you experience emotional and spiritual healing—and even perhaps physical healing—as a result of your new, improved relationship with the loving consciousness of creation.

A better relationship with Source can provide many benefits.

Your God-and-Religion Story

Identifying your story about God and religion can be an important first step in deepening your spirituality and developing a better relationship with Source. Maybe your God-and-religion story is one of the following:

- The thought of a God who looks out for me and answers prayers is comforting, but my logic and reason tell me that there is no God, so I'm not a believer.
- I am not religious so much as spiritual, and I believe in a Higher Power, but I'm not quite sure exactly what I believe. Plus, I don't have many—and maybe, not any—spiritual practices that help me feel connected to this Higher Power.
- I identify with a particular religion. I believe in God and try to follow my religion's teachings, but often, they don't speak to my heart and soul, so I would like to further explore my spirituality.

Or is your God-and-religion story perhaps something else? You can write a brief description of your story about God and religion and fill in the statements below. If you have trouble identifying your story, you might use a hidden-wisdom technique to learn more about it and then try to put your story into words.

My story about God and religion is: _____

_____

_____

_____

Looking at my story about God and religion, if there is anything that I would like to change, it is this: _____

_____

_____

_____

_____

I would like to make this change because: _____

_____

_____

_____

The origin of the parts of my spiritual story that I want to change is: _____

_____

_____

_____

These parts of my God-and-religion story that I'd like to change have been reinforced and validated by: _____

_____

_____

_____

If anything has held me back from examining and consciously changing my story about God and religion, it is: _____

_____

_____

_____

It's common to fear that something bad will happen to you if you question religious teachings that you were expected to adopt. If you have friends, relatives and a community that want you to hold certain beliefs and values and accept certain religious teachings, it might be hard for you to explore your story about God and religion and the possibility of changing it.

You might want to get in touch with your hidden wisdom to learn more about your story of God and religion and perhaps dialogue with your wise inner self or your religion. If you decide to use a hidden-wisdom technique to gain insights and energies for transforming your story of God and religion to be one that is more pleasing to you and to Source, you can write about that experience here.

When using a hidden-wisdom technique to learn more about my story of God and religion, this is what I experienced and learned: _____

_____

_____

_____

_____

_____

_____

_____

_____

You might want to get in touch with your hidden wisdom to learn more about your story of God and religion and perhaps dialogue with your wise inner self or your religion.

How Nature Helps You Feel More Connected to Source

Our modern lifestyles often cause us to feel disconnected from nature. We check a smart phone to find out what the weather is rather than open a door or a window. We spend much of our time working or studying indoors. Because of this disconnection, we can suffer health problems and mood difficulties. However, if we reconnect with nature, we can not only improve our moods and even our health but feel a closer connection to Source.

The relaxed state you create when you are by a lake, in some woods, or even simply enjoying a walk through a garden will make it easier to ignore distractions, open to your hidden wisdom, and feel the presence of Source. Then you might want to take a seat and observe nature. You might pose to nature the question, *Are you observing me as I observe you?* If you feel the answer is *yes*, you can ask any of the following:

- *Why are you observing me?*
- *What are you seeing?*
- *How are you able to see what is going on with me?*

Maybe nature sees your best aspects and your potential. Maybe nature wants you to see what she sees. Or maybe Source is making these observations through nature. I talk to nature as if she were a living entity because I believe she and Source are inseparable. You might want to tell the flowers how beautiful they are and tell the pine trees how good being among them makes you feel. Or you might simply want to thank Source for creating nature and express to Source why you're grateful for the plants, the birds, and so on.

As you stroll along the banks of a river or through a forest, you might experience spiritual truths found in various traditions. One such truth is that nature continues no matter what happens—that things are born as others die. Another is that we are interconnected within the natural environment—you can recognize this as you see birds swoop down to snatch fish from below the surface of the water or a squirrel with a nut disappear into the hollow space in a dead tree. Nature is also collaborative. You can observe this as you see the plants feeding the animals, who will die and have their bodies become food for plants. You might not realize this, but even trees are collaborative: They speak to each other by sending chemical signals through their roots into the soil they share with other trees and plants. If one of their fellow trees is suffering, they will send nutrients to help it. It seems they do not see other trees as competition for nutrients but as siblings that collaborate with them in providing shade, shelter, and nourishment for insects and creatures—and us.

Contemplating nature's lessons can help you recognize your interconnectedness with Source, and help you see that perhaps the trees or natural world might help you if you're suffering, just as they help each other. You might recall people you've interacted with who helped you in some away, a reminder that we can count on Source to send us resources that include people— even strangers—who are willing to assist us.

Nature reinforces your hidden wisdom about the nature of life itself. Seeing connections among the chapters of your life might be easier when you're outdoors among the trees and birds. Letting go of a grudge—allowing it to die or pruning it away to allow your energy to flow toward more fruitful thoughts—can become easier after you soak in nature's lessons about death and vitality. In nature, you recognize that there are seasons and cycles. These are a reminder that your life has seasons and cycles, too, and that when you're feeling you're in a winter-like period of scarcity, Source may not be neglecting you so much as challenging you to find ways to help yourself during a cycle in which you aren't experiencing joy and abundance.

Whether or not we consciously recognize nature's lessons, we absorb them. I think they will always be there for us but can become hidden within us. We may have to slow down and use a hidden-wisdom technique to tap into that wisdom, allowing us to more easily bring about changes in our day-to-day lives.

When we're in touch with our spirituality, we remember that our true nature or soul is always interconnected with nature and the wisdom we can tap into when we're feeling connected to it. The hidden-wisdom practices in this book can help you draw in insights and energy for transformation from nature itself. Outdoors, you might remember the wisdom to go with the flow, like a leaf on the surface of a river, and even deeply internalize that message.

Keeping all the benefits of time in nature in your mind, you might want to find ways to use hidden-wisdom techniques outdoors in natural spaces rather than indoors.

Nature and Mental and Physical Health

I am in awe of nature's ability to affect us at the physical, psychological, spiritual, and energetic levels. Being in nature, observing its rhythms and habits and contemplating its lessons, feeds and reveals our hidden wisdom. Nature tends to relativize our problems for us: Obstacles don't seem so daunting after all. We remember that we don't have to rely solely on our analytical minds to solve problems. We remember that nature is teeming with wisdom, and we become less fearful or melancholy.

In addition to relaxing us, nature influences us through what we eat. Healthy, natural foods such as blueberries and broccoli can turn on cellular repair systems in our body and even impact our genetic expression. Genes for disease might not express after all, allowing us to enjoy good health for a longer time than we would if we were to eat unhealthy, unnatural foods. You might say that plants share with us their wisdom for how to remain healthy. I think instinctively we know that fruits and vegetables are better for us than fast food!

Spending time in nature reduces your amount of stress hormones, improves your immunity, bathes you in sunlight that raises your vitamin D levels, and seems to reduce the risk of developing nearsightedness. Our bodies and spirits seem to thrive when we spend time near bodies of water, under vast skies, and near trees, grass, and brush. Nature is, after all, our original home. The health benefits of being *home* are so great that some physicians are even prescribing nature walks for their patients.

Nature seems to recalibrate us, bringing us back to the rhythm and flow of our bodies' natural home outdoors. Nature can bring us back into our bodies and reconnect us with ourselves. We evolved to be outdoors, sharing the planet with plants, insects, and other creatures, with our feet on the earth and our eyes scanning the distance as well as seeing what is right in front of us. We are meant to hear sounds surrounding us, traveling to our ears from near and far and above and below.

Very quickly after we enter a natural outdoor space, natural sounds such as the wind swooshing through trees and water softly sloshing against the shore of a lake can actually cause our nervous system to switch into a repair mode, relaxing us. And according to scientific research, we can achieve the same effect merely by listening to recordings of natural sounds. Nature's influence is that powerful!

Studies show we can experience health *and* psychological benefits if we spend time practicing *shin-rin yoku* or forest bathing, that is, if we immerse ourselves in a forest.

Twenty or thirty minutes spent in natural surroundings will not only reduce your body's levels of the stress hormone cortisol, showing that your parasympathetic nervous system (calming and repair system) is active, but will likely give you a sense of well-being. Exercise has the same effect, which is why getting out into nature for a walk doubles the support you can give your body in recovering from everyday stressors.

Doing Rituals and Using Hidden-Wisdom Techniques Outdoors in Nature

Doing rituals or using hidden-wisdom techniques in nature can make them even more powerful, intensifying your experience of nourishing your hidden wisdom and gaining insights and energy for change. Try it for yourself and see whether it helps you feel in touch with your spirituality and more connected to Source.

Hidden-Wisdom Techniue: Engaging Nature for Wisdom

To tap into wisdom beyond your own, you might want to plan to engage nature in a place where you won't be interrupted. Once you are by the roots of a particular tree or seated in a grassy spot on a riverbank, or in any other natural place that calls to you, listen to your instincts about how you might work with nature. Sit and focus on the experience of the earth beneath you, the wind and sky surrounding you, the sun warming your skin, and the smells of forest, river, or sea entering your nostrils. Allow your senses to fully awaken as you adjust to the sounds and rhythms of the space. Focus on the sensations you're experiencing. In this way, you open yourself up to the subtle energies that can wash out of you what is no longer needed, infuse you, and heal you. Let nature do what it needs to do to the energy that enlivens your body and causes your cells to reproduce and do the work of keeping you alive.

You might walk and gaze at trees, perhaps noticing branches that are thriving as well as ones that have broken. Notice the pattern of the tree's bark or its branches. Touch the bark or leaves if you can and notice how it feels. As you look at the silhouette of that lone tree against a blue sky, or you listen to the buzz of insects or observe water tumbling over rocks in a creek or river, notice whether a particular thought or emotion arises.

Find a comfortable spot and set an intention to learn from nature. If you like, be specific in shaping that intention. Maybe you'd like to know how you can solve a particular problem or gain insights into a situation that's puzzling to you. Maybe you'd like help in making an important decision.

Once your intention is set, sit with your eyes open, continuing to focus on the sights, sounds, and smells all around you. Some of these sensations may be quite subtle, but if you're quiet and willing to pay attention, you can pick up on them. If you see an animal or an insect such as a moth or butterfly, watch its movements. Take time to look at each plant or tree. Notice what's on the ground. Is there water nearby? In a puddle or in the sky in the form of a cloud? Observe it. You might come to experience an insight from your inner wisdom that rises to the surface because of something you're observing in this spot.

Open yourself to any messages from nature that come to you as an inner knowing, some words, a metaphor, or a synchronicity (a meaningful coincidence). You might ponder what you can learn from the sound of a bird calling as it perches in a tree before taking flight or what meaning there might be in a bird taking flight just as a cloud covers the sun—is it a synchronicity?

After at least fifteen minutes in nature, check in with yourself. Notice whether you have a different perspective on your life, whether problems that seemed too burdensome now are somewhat relativized, helping you to feel more hopeful about working through them.

If something has changed in your surroundings since you began observing nature, such as the temperature or the light, pay attention to how you responded to those changes. You might want to answer the following questions.

If you observed changes in nature while engaging it for wisdom, how did you feel about the changes and what did you make of them? For example, did they reveal to you an answer to a question you posed or give you insights about a problem you intended to learn about?

_____

_____

_____

_____

If something unexpected happened as you sat observing, what was it, how did you feel about it, and did it provide any insights or answers related to what it is you intended to learn about?

_____

_____

_____

_____

If you felt bored or restless while observing nature, why do you think that is? What might that boredom or restlessness be telling you—for example, is it answering a question you posed or shedding light on a topic of concern you intended to learn about? _____

_____

_____

_____

Next, if you like, you can dialogue with nature to learn any lessons she can teach you, including lessons about your boredom and restlessness. If you do this, you might want to record your experience below.

My experience dialoguing with nature: _____

_____

_____

_____

_____

_____

_____

_____

_____

_____

_____

You might try this exercise more than once and see if you get different answers by dialoguing with nature herself or a part of nature, such as the sky or a tree. Whatever you experience while dialoguing, be sure to act upon any insights you have gained. In this way, nature can be healing not just for your body but for your emotional self and even your spirit. Nature can offer you wisdom that will actually lead to changes in your life. You might find it easier to make some decisions or to manage difficult situations and put them in perspective, all thanks to the insights and energy exchange you experienced while engaging and dialoguing with nature.

Ayni and Nature

Ayni is a word in the Quechua language of the Q'ero people of Peru. It means reciprocity or harmony. Nature gives to us—air for us to breathe, water for us to drink, food for us to eat, medicinal plants, and more. Do we reciprocate by offering something to her? Doing so shows respect and can help you feel more connected to nature and to all living things—and all consciousness. You might thank nature after you do hidden-wisdom work outdoors. You might plant seeds, release a leaf or twig into the current of a creek, or skip a stone into the water, or volunteer for a forest restoration project to express your respect for nature.

Special Places in Nature

Many different wisdom traditions have recognized that natural spaces can affect people's energy in particular ways. There are sacred spaces on earth that ancient people recognized as having special powers for healing and transformation, such as the energy vortexes in Sedona, Arizona. Perhaps Stonehenge was built where it was because long ago, people recognized it as a spot rich in healing energies. If you visit a power place, such as a vortex, you can soak in energy that will replenish you when you're feeling drained and lethargic or release energies that are weighing you down with worry or grief.

Whether or not you visit such places, when you feel overstimulated by all that is happening in your environment and in your mind, you might want to go to a forest, lake, desert, or some other natural area. You'll probably find that soon you begin to feel a shift in your awareness and mood as you become balanced and refreshed. If you sense your intuition start to awaken, listen to it.

Maybe you're sensitive enough to recognize the subtle changes in energy as you walk from one area in this natural space to another. If not, you might be able to develop this ability by spending more time in nature.

You might also be able to find special natural places with healing power on your own, allowing your intuition to guide you. Once, a friend of mine who is a shaman in Peru invited me to explore and walk around the land behind his home. "Go where you need to be," he told me. "Let the earth heal you." I set out to wander around his land and walked until I suddenly felt compelled to lie down on the grass under a tree. I lay there until I felt replenished and then arose to see him approaching me with a smile.

"That's a natural balancing spot," he told me. "Many of my visitors have been drawn to that very place."

Try to explore natural areas, away from the distractions of everyday modern life and away from the energy fields of electronic equipment that might interfere with your ability to tap into nature's energies. You may find that simply being in your yard, near a public garden, or in a particular spot by a river where you feel drawn to sit for a while helps you to reconnect to the balancing, healing energies of nature.

Exercise: Writing Poetry or Drawing in a Natural Spot That Attracts You

You might want to go to a natural area with this workbook and a pen and allow yourself to be drawn to a spot that feels like the right place to sit and take in the energy of the space. If you do, give yourself some time before writing about your experience. Be fully present, savoring and observing this natural space. Then you might want to write a poem about what you're seeing and experiencing. Your poem might rhyme, or it might not. It might be a haiku, with five syllables in the first line, seven in the next, and five in the third and last line. If you don't feel like composing a poem, you might want to draw a picture inspired by your natural surroundings. Let your imagination run free as you connect with how you feel in that restorative place in nature and aim to express it.

Here's a poem I wrote about Source after being inspired by nature. Maybe it will inspire your own poem or drawing.

On Serving Source
The rocks are patient, very patient.
They are aware of almost everything.
Since the beginning,
they noted the frenetic, ephemeral activities of humans.
When asked if it hurts to be carved,
they answer, "No.
We are what we are, our essence unchanging."
The rocks are very quiet and bring love.

The plants love to dance in the wind,
aware that they help Source with creation. They are happy to play, give beauty,
and offer themselves up for nourishment to all creatures.
They shine love.

The animals know they represent wondrous diversity
Jaguar, antelope, bee, zebra, snail,
cricket, starfish, mongoose, eel—
all so separate but alike.
They are great teachers for those open to learn
and in their way, they teach love.

The human beings, the awakened ones,
are here to serve Source,
to help bring into being what does not yet exist
except in the Quiet.

They contain the energy and essence of the rocks,
the plants, and the animals.
Their diversity is infinite, and in constant interplay,
searching for ayni, right relationship.
When humans, too, can truly love
then hallelujah, hallelujah.

God, Source, consciousness, life indwells
but is only experienced, never completely known.
She, he, we are to be celebrated and honored
and we need to serve others and life
with love and intent.

What I want to say/draw/express about a restorative place in nature:

Let yourself be drawn to natural spaces where you can engage energy that will balance and refresh you.

How You Can Commune with Nature Despite Limitations

If there's no way for you to get outdoors due to a medical or health condition, you can still receive the gifts of nature. When using hidden-wisdom techniques, you might want to find a spot indoors where you can look out into a natural area through a window. You might also want to open a window to hear natural sounds such as wind rustling the leaves of a tree or birds singing.

Playing recordings of nature sounds or watching nature videos can help you relax and boost your mood. It's been found that nature sounds increase the productivity of office workers.

You might also switch your computer's screensaver or phone's wallpaper to a view of the clouds or a sunset. You could take breaks during your workday to watch videos of a crackling fire, a frozen river beginning to thaw, or jellyfish undulating in an aquarium. You might decide that when you're waiting for an appointment and have some extra time, instead of looking at a newsfeed, you'll watch a video of prairie grass swaying in the wind or the sun peeking out from behind a cloud.

Why not bring more plants into the spaces where you live, work, or study, or at least have photographs or images of natural scenes? Then too, animals can help you feel your connection to nature. Cats, dogs, birds, and fish might help you feel more relaxed and connected to the matrix of creation and living creatures, alleviating loneliness and reminding you to slow down and enjoy life. You can feel a sense of purpose in supporting your pet. Some would even say that pets offer us wisdom by unconditionally loving us. Wherever you are, you can find a way to connect with nature—or with Source.

A Goal for Connecting with Nature and with Spirit

If you want to spend more time in nature—or use a spiritual practice to feel more connected to Source—you could set a goal around that.

Keeping in mind the need for accountability, I'm setting this specific, achievable goal for more time in nature and/or more time connected to Source: _____

_____

_____

_____

_____

I achieved my goal: Yes No (Circle one)

Any notes on what helped or hindered me in trying to reach my goal: _____

_____

_____

_____

_____

Speaking of healing, in the next chapter, you'll be doing some exercises to gain wisdom about any health issues you might be having. Your body has wisdom that might be hidden from your awareness, and all you have learned so far can help you to access that wisdom and use it to improve your health.

Chapter 14
Hidden Wisdom About Health

The story of your health is a chapter in the larger story of your life, but it's helpful to look at it as a story itself. Once you identify it, you can consciously change it if it's not pleasing to you. And just as with the story of your life, your hidden wisdom can help you to write a new and better health story and bring it to life.

Often, we don't think about our health until something goes wrong. Maybe we develop a medical condition or an accident injures us. Maybe it isn't our own health crisis that turns our attention to our health story but something that happens to somebody else. When a close friend dies from a lifestyle-related cause, and your lifestyle is similar to theirs, you might recognize for the first time what you knew intellectually but never emotionally processed: that your own health and safety is at risk because of your choices.

You might also be aging but not want to think of yourself as old or even getting older. Others may be more focused on your health than you are. All our stories are influenced by other people's stories and ideas about us. Are people telling you to "take it easy" or "watch your step" because they assume your balance isn't what it used to be or because a disease you have makes balance challenging at times? Maybe they are onto something and it's best not to be defensive. Maybe you should examine the chapter on balance within the story of your health. You'll learn more about these chapters shortly.

Western medicine tends to treat health mechanistically. If a system isn't working, you get surgery or take a medication to fix it. However, if we look at health holistically, as many other cultures do, we might find that our health problems mirror challenges we have in other areas of our lives. An autoimmune disorder occurs when the body doesn't recognize its own cells and, in its confusion, attacks them. I'm not saying that an experience of not being able to maintain good boundaries with others or being highly empathetic causes autoimmune disorders. I'm saying that it could be helpful to think thematically about any diseases or conditions you have and see if those themes show up in other areas of your life. It's possible that by addressing the theme as it plays out in your relationships or your career you might lessen then symptoms of your disease or condition.

Discovering Your Health Story

If you discover your health story is a negative one, keep this in mind: Studies show that people who have a positive attitude about aging live longer, experience better health as they age, and have a lower risk of developing dementia. And as you work with the exercises in this chapter, remember that archetypal energies you encounter and bring into your energy field to influence you can fade away if you don't set goals for change and stick to them.

Often, we don't think about our health until something goes wrong.

In Chapter 5, you identified your life story up until this point and any changes you want to make in the health chapter. While it's good to have some specific goals regarding your health, let's go a little deeper now and try to identify your health story because it may be preventing you from experiencing better health. Even if you end up not being able to change your health situation as much as you would like, you can relate to a health condition or aging differently, which can reduce its negative influence on your mood or quality of life.

Here are some health stories you might be holding onto that might be keeping you from better health whether or not you're conscious of them:

- *I just want my health problems fixed so I can get back to my old life. I don't know how to fix them, so I want someone else to do it for me.*

- *I don't have time to eat right, get enough sleep, or exercise, and I'm scared!*

- *I don't need to think about my health story for a long time. I'm healthy enough today not to make a big deal about a few health problems and some bad health habits.*

- *I'm getting older, which means my health will fail soon. There's not much I can do to prevent that.*

Maybe your health story is that you're a cancer patient, a cancer warrior, a cancer survivor, or someone who has had cancer or is living with cancer. How you frame your cancer experience is up to you.

You could be holding on to a health story such as, *I'm always waiting for the other shoe to drop. I don't trust that I can really stay cancer free (or keep the cancer in check) for a long time. It'll get me in the end.* You might want to replace it with a health story such as:

- *I'm a cancer survivor, but I don't want my experience with the disease to be such a dominant part of my life. I want to move on to focusing on some other aspect of my life and maybe set some goals I was afraid to set before when I had to focus on surviving cancer.*

- *I'm doing everything I can to avoid having the cancer come back (or avoid developing cancer), and this journey has offered me many gifts. It's helped me make new friends and feel a sense of purpose.*

If your health story is disempowering because you're aging or have health problems, you might want to write and adopt a health story such as:

- *I'm not getting older. I'm getting better! I'm developing greater wisdom and peace than I had in my younger years, and the tradeoff of having some health conditions or aches and pains that I've been unable to get rid of completely is worth it. Besides, maybe I can reduce my aches and pains by making some changes.*

- *I'm healing and getting stronger and healthier in ways I never thought possible or necessary. As a result, I'm happier and more contented than I have ever been.*

Remember what I said about the power of the mind when it adopts a positive attitude toward aging. You can adopt a positive attitude toward managing an autoimmune disorder, fighting a disease, or restoring your health to a set point you enjoyed in the past.

Hidden Obstacles to Optimal Health

Coming to peace with the uncertainty of not knowing what the future holds, resolving unfinished business that might be causing you stress, and developing a deeper relationship with Source can all be ways of healing that may affect your ability to achieve physical healing. For example, any of these changes might relieve symptoms of a health condition. Even if the healing is only psychological and spiritual, it can be profound. People I have talked to who have had to face the possibility of death from a disease have told me that working with hidden wisdom, and discovering obstacles they weren't aware of, has allowed them to heal their fears such as, *What will happen to my kids if I die?*, and better face their health challenges. It's also helped them heal wounds from old hurts that occurred in their relationships, allowing them to both forgive others and say, *I'm sorry. Please forgive me*, which has led to a sense of peace. And working with hidden wisdom has also helped them to experience their interconnectedness with Source and feel more confident that even if they were to die, they would continue to live in some form.

Maybe something within you needs to be healed for you to fully release any obstacles to living a healthy, happy, fulfilling life, one in which you don't feel you're missing anything. Whatever is unhealed or absent from your life could be contributing to any health problems you're having. I've known people whose health improved after they let go of stressors that they understood were probably having some effect on their health but didn't recognize were a major cause of their health problems. Better relationships and a deeper connection to Spirit might help you become healthier. We know that loneliness and a lack of strong social connections in older people is correlated with obesity, Alzheimer's disease, heart disease, high blood pressure, low immunity, anxiety and depression, and an earlier death. Experiencing your connection with Spirit can help you to feel less alone and give you the courage to work on your relationships to make them more enriching.

While in the West, we tend to separate physical health from mental, emotional, and spiritual health (feeling a sense of purpose and connection), I believe they're all intertwined. I've often found that if you work on some health ailment by accessing your hidden wisdom and interacting with energies in your unconscious that are affecting you, you can be surprised at the results. You might find you don't have that ailment anymore, or you only rarely experience it. You might also find you've healed yourself in some other way—for example, you might have let go of your fear that you're getting older and "it's all downhill from here." Similarly, working on any of the other chapters of your story, or on your life story, might result in experiencing better health. There are many sub-chapters in your story's health chapter that you can work on or that might improve as a side-benefit from doing hidden wisdom work:

- Eating, drinking, and weight

- Balance

- Movement/exercise

- Flexibility

- Stamina

- Sexuality

- Body image

- Changes due to hormonal shifts (such as menopause or andropause)

- Management of an acute or chronic condition

- Fatigue

Any of these chapters can have themes that you find in another chapter of your life or health. For example, earlier, I mentioned having strong boundaries with others. If you don't have them, you might want to think about how that affects the chapters of your health story. You might find yourself with poor stamina, feeling fatigued, when you're once again expected to be an emotional caretaker for someone in your family who is very needy. Your emotional fatigue might show up as physical fatigue. So, as you read the list of health story chapters, think metaphorically. If you're having trouble with physical flexibility, you might be experiencing rigidity and a lack of flow in some other area of your life.

Maybe something within you needs to be healed for you to fully release any obstacles to living a healthy, happy, fulfilling life.

Your Genes Don't Have to Determine Your Health Story

Discovering that you have or might have a gene associated with health problems can be frightening or upsetting, but you are the storyteller of your life. You don't have to live according to the dictates of a health story written for you by your DNA, your past experiences and actions, or your conditioning. You can do much to change the story of your health, including using the mind/body connection and making lifestyle changes that can help your body not to express genes for disease.

On one hand, you might say, *I come from a family where most of the women have died of heart disease before turning 60. Because I'm a woman, that will probably be my fate. There's not much I can do about it, especially since heart disease is in my genes.* Consider how that story may have an energetic influence on you. Then, think about how much better the energetic influence might be if you wrote this story instead: *I come from a family where many of the women have died of heart disease before they turned 60, but I'm not going to be one of those statistics. I'm going to exercise more, better manage my stress, and clean up my diet, which will help me to beat those odds and give me a better chance of living beyond 60. I choose to do what I can so that any genes for heart disease don't get expressed.*

We're still learning the mechanisms that might explain the well-documented, powerful correlations between optimism and better health outcomes and reduced symptoms of diseases and conditions. However, we do know that thoughts and emotions can affect our bodies positively and negatively. For example, humorous thoughts that make you laugh have the power to generate endorphins, neurotransmitters that reduce pain and set off a biological stress response that leads to the repair of damaged cells. It's possible that other types of thoughts and emotions set off a positive chain reaction that affects your physical state and even your gene expression.

Thoughts and emotions can affect our bodies positively and negatively.

Further Exploring Your Health Story

Many people intend to someday change their bad habits regarding their health or another chapter of their story, but that day never comes—or it does, but only after a problem has developed. To write and bring to life a better story of your health*, consider using a hidden-wisdom technique to learn more about your health story as it is. For example, you could take a Journey to the Room of Contracts to Change a Hidden Belief related to your health story, do the Visualization to Observe Yourself in the Past, or do the Visualization of a Future Day. You can do a dialogue during these journeys or visualizations, or afterward, and you can also try to identify your stories about specific chapters of your health story. Even if you feel pretty sure you know what your health story is, I encourage you to use a hidden-wisdom technique to learn more—and then record your experiences and insights here.

The hidden-wisdom technique I used to learn more about my health story as it is—and what I experienced: _____

_____

_____

_____

_____

_____

_____

_____

My old health story was: _____

_____

_____

_____

---

* If you would like to work further with your health story, you might want to look at my book *Change the Story of Your Health: Using Jungian and Shamanic Techniques for Healing.*

Any actions I know I want take to let go of the old health story: _____

_____

_____

_____

_____

What about a new health story? What would you like it to be? You might want to think about your experiences and beliefs about what you'll experience in the future regarding the chapters within it. Again, they are:

- Eating, drinking, and weight
- Balance
- Movement/exercise
- Flexibility
- Stamina
- Sexuality
- Body image
- Changes due to hormonal shifts (such as menopause or andropause)
- Management of an acute or chronic condition
- Fatigue

And again, think thematically and metaphorically when you consider these chapters, reflecting on where you're not experiencing balance, stamina, the ability to manage challenges or changes, etc.

You might want to answer the following questions, focusing on one chapter from this list or choosing a combination of related chapters. Movement and exercise, flexibility, and stamina could be a grouping, and sexuality, body image, and changes due to hormonal shifts could be another.

When it comes to your health story, or a particular chapter or group of chapters within it, what is working for you? For example, do you have good habits you'd like to maintain? Are you having good health experiences you want to continue having? _____

_____

_____

_____

_____

What is not working for you when it comes to your health story or a particular chapter of it (or group of chapters within it)? For example, are there new habits you'd like to adopt to replace old habits that are contributing to your health problems? _____

_____

_____

_____

_____

_____

As you look at what isn't working for you, when did these problems or habits originate? What else was happening in your life at the time? _____

_____

_____

_____

_____

Do you see a connection between what was happening in your life at the time and the health story you want to change? Circle one: Yes No

If so, what's the connection? For example, are there habits that are causing you health problems and that are related to a relationship breakup, an especially stressful time at work, etc.?

_____

_____

_____

_____

Do you see any connections among your current habits and any problems you're having with your health? Circle one: Yes No

If so, what are the habits and health problems? _____

_____

_____

_____

_____

Any events, or messages you received from others or the culture you grew up in, that might have influenced your health story: _____

_____

_____

_____

_____

If you haven't changed health habits that you say you would like to change, why do you think that is? _____

_____

_____

_____

What I would like my new health story to be: _____

_____

_____

_____

If you want to set a concrete goal for changing your health story, you can write it here and come back to it later to be sure you hold yourself accountable for attaining that goal.

My specific, achievable goal for making a change in my health habits or practices contributing to health or illness is: _____

_____

_____

_____

I achieved my goal: Yes No (Circle one)

Any notes on what helped or hindered me in trying to reach my goal: _____

_____

_____

_____

_____

If you have assumed you can't experience significant improvements in your health, question that assumption. Science and research are constantly changing. You never know when new treatments for a health condition might become available. You might not realize there are simple changes you can make to your health habits that will make a noticeable difference in your health and how you feel—for example, no longer drinking sweetened beverages or stretching for just two or three minutes a day. Remember, you can always make incremental changes that will set you on the course to bigger changes—and more noticeable results.

Try reading aloud your new health story and noticing how you feel about it. Remember, positive emotions and attitudes toward aging and health can contribute to your bringing to life a new and better health story.

If you have assumed you can't experience significant improvements in your health, question that assumption.

And even if you only set one goal for change to bring about a better health story, remember: One small change can lead to another and, eventually, to a big change.

The chapters of our life story tend to overlap. When you consider the chapters of your health story metaphorically, you might see struggles with balance, movement, stamina, flexibility, and so on in your relationships, your work life, your psychology, or your relationship with Spirit. For example, maybe you don't balance work and home life well *and* you have physical balance problems. This might cause problems in your relationships and at your job even as you struggle with the challenge of poor physical balance. Maybe you have trouble with physical *and* emotional stamina and flexibility, causing difficulties in your marriage and in your work life. Maybe you're pushing yourself too hard at work, and you're in a romantic relationship that has a lot of problems, and your migraines or backaches began around the time demands at work and conflicts with your partner increased.

As I said, it's possible that by improving on one chapter of your story you'll bring about positive changes in another. To help you see connections among emotions, physical health, and mindsets or attitudes, consider answering the following questions.

Is there a chapter in your health story that mirrors another chapter in your life story, and if so, what are those chapters and the connections? For example, do you have a poor body image and a poor self-image overall that affects your relationships, or a lack of physical and emotional balance that shows up in your relationships and work life? _____

_____

_____

_____

_____

If you would like to address a health problem that is mirrored in another area of your life, what is it and how would you like to address it? _____

_____

_____

_____

_____

If you want to set a concrete goal for changing a particular issue, which may be related to balance, body image, etc., you can write it here and come back to it later to be sure you hold yourself accountable for attaining it.

🎯 **Keeping in mind accountability, my specific, achievable goal for changing an issue that's affecting my health chapter and at least one other chapter in my story is:** _____

_____

_____

_____

_____

✔️ **I achieved my goal:** Yes No (Circle one)

Any notes on what helped or hindered me in trying to reach my goal: _____

_____

_____

_____

_____

Hidden-Wisdom Technique: Journey to the Upper World to See Your Future Health

The shamans of Peru that I have worked with believe that if you can journey to an invisible realm called the upper world, you can learn about your future. This hidden-wisdom technique is based on their practice. You can use it to learn about your health in the future or any other aspect of your life. As always, during the journey, you might experience an exchange of energy if you realize you must let go of something and bring something else into your life. And you'll encounter a guardian whose permission to journey you'll want to receive and who will accompany you.

In this particular journey, you'll ascend a mountain and enter four different caves along the path toward the top. In each, you'll pose a question for your hidden wisdom to answer.

In the first cave, it will be: *What will my health be like in five or ten years if I do nothing now to change my habits?*

In the second, it will be: *What do I need to let go of to improve my health so that I don't experience what I saw in my future when I was in the previous cave?*

In the third, it will be: *What do I need to bring in to improve my health so that I don't experience what I saw in my future when I was in the first cave?*

In the fourth, it will be: *If I make the changes I just learned about, what will my health look like in five years?*

You will encounter the answers in the caves—and before leaving each, you'll ask if there's anything else you need to know before you go on to the next cave.

When the journey is over and you've finished at the last cave, you will make your way down to the base of the mountain, accompanied by your guardian, who has been with you all the time. There, you'll stop to feel the power of what you experienced before you say good-bye and thank you to your guardian, at which point you will end your journey and return to ordinary consciousness.

Start the journey by setting aside a time to get quiet, relax, and take yourself into a meditative state so that you can more easily tap into your hidden wisdom and receive its messages.

Script for the Journey to the Upper World to See Your Future Health

Imagine a mountain before you, one that holds great wisdom it wants to share with you. Feel yourself beginning to ascend it by climbing a path that winds clockwise around this mountain. With effort but not straining yourself, you climb until you see before you a cave you can enter …

Pause before this cave. Notice that your wise inner self, your guardian, who wants only the best for you appears. Ask, *Is today a good time for me to continue my journey to the upper world to learn about my future health?* If the guardian says yes, offer thanks and continue. If it says no, ask, *What do I need to do to make this journey safe for me?* Wait for the answer. It could be something like, *Be open to what you will learn even if it makes you uncomfortable,* or *Don't turn on your analytical mind to figure out the messages you receive. Simply receive them and know that you can later intuit and ponder their meaning. That way, you're more likely to fully understand the message.* If you don't receive permission despite your willingness to do something for your wise inner self, offer thanks for the protection, walk back down the mountain, and return to an ordinary state of consciousness, knowing you can try again another day …

When you receive permission to continue your journey, ask your hidden wisdom, *What will my health be like in five years if I do nothing now to change my habits?* Then, pause until the time feels right to enter the cave, where you'll receive an answer in some form …

After receiving the answer, ask your hidden wisdom, *Is there anything else I need to know before I leave this cave?* Again, wait for the answer … When you're ready, leave the cave, rejoin your guardian, and ascend the mountain to the next cave …

At the second cave, repeat this inquiry process, asking the question, *What do I need to let go of to improve my health so that I don't experience what I saw in my future when I was in the previous cave?* Enter the cave and wait for the answer … Then ask if there is anything else you need to know before leaving the cave. For example, you may need to release an energy of denial or anger about your health condition because it's keeping you from making needed changes to your habits. As always, when you learn what you need to release, you can choose to do it in your imagination or by using your hands to sweep energy out of you and away from you …

When you've received your answer about what to release, and you feel ready to continue your journey, rejoin your guardian and ascend the mountain to the third cave … At the third cave's entrance, repeat your inquiry process, asking, *What do I need to bring in to improve my health so that I don't experience what I saw in my future when I was in the first cave?* Enter the cave and receive the answer …

Again, you can use your imagination or your hands to sweep into yourself a new energy. Before departing the cave, remember to ask if there's anything else you need to know …

When you rejoin your wise inner self, ascend to the final, fourth cave. Stand before it and ask, *If I make the changes I just learned about, what will my health look like in five years?* Again, enter the cave and wait for the answer … After receiving the answer, ask if there's anything else you need to know before departing …

When you're ready, exit the cave and descend the mountain with your guardian at your side … At the bottom of the mountain, pause as you absorb the wisdom you received … Thank your guardian for its help and thank your hidden wisdom for its guidance. Then, when you're ready, open your eyes and re-enter an ordinary mind state.

If you took an upper world journey, you can write here about your experience.

My experience with the hidden-wisdom technique of journeying to the upper world and its four caves of wisdom to learn about my future health and how I can affect it was this: _____

_____

_____

_____

_____

Having taken the upper world journey, you might want to set a concrete goal for changing your health story. If so, you can write it here and come back to it later to be sure you hold yourself accountable for attaining that goal.

🎯 **Keeping in mind the need for accountability, I'm setting this specific, achievable goal for making a change so I experience better health in the future:** _____

_____

_____

_____

_____

✔ **I achieved my goal:** Yes No (Circle one)

Any notes on what helped or hindered me in trying to reach my goal: _____

_____

_____

_____

_____

A Balance Between Battling Toxins and Building Immunity

Determined to live long and healthy lives, many of us go to war against germs and viruses that can jeopardize our health and well-being. But how often do we consider creating a balance between battling toxins and building immunity?

To destroy biological invaders in your body, you might take antibiotics or other medications that can have strong side effects. Uncomfortable though you may be with the gastrointestinal disturbances, headaches, or other symptoms of a war being waged within you, you might be so focused on getting well again that you forget to consider how those toxins and bacteria entered your system in the first place. How did they come to find sanctuary within you?

You can't eradicate every germ, virus, or bacteria toxin that enters your body. However, you might be able to stop them from moving in and putting their feet up on the coffee table, so to speak. Your immune system might be weak and need to be built up so that your system can kill them off quickly.

Eating large quantities of sugar, whether as sweets or processed flour in breads and cereals, can weaken your ability to maintain strong immunity. Indulging in these carbohydrates can cause you to lay out a banquet for yeast and bacteria to feed upon. Then you battle infections or struggle with your weight. But much of that fighting would not be necessary if you were willing to avoid these foods and do a better job building and maintaining a strong immune system.

Building immunity requires consuming fewer foods that your system has trouble processing and getting rid of while favoring foods that support your health. Green, leafy vegetables, healthy sources of proteins such as nuts and seeds, and fermented foods are all known to support strong immunity. Adding these foods to your diet can help you to be prepared for the inevitable invasion of toxins and battles necessary for staying healthy. If you lie to yourself about what you're consuming, you get stuck having to wage unnecessary wars and wishing your immune systems were stronger. Illness and even chronic disease can result.

Your body has cancer cells, viruses, bacteria, and even toxic manmade chemicals within it that will threaten your health if you aren't vigilant. You can tolerate a certain amount of assaults against your natural state of health. After too many attacks, your body can't keep up the fight. Building your immunity when it's weak gives your body more power to wage important battles. You can choose to keep your body in better shape for overpowering a virus quickly or healing an infection that begins to develop.

As you think about your own body's fitness for battle, think about how prepared you are for doing the hard work of maintaining or even improving your health and well-being. Maybe you work at it daily, or maybe you do very little to support your health and simply wait for something to go wrong before you attend to it.

If you consciously choose to find a balance between doing battle and building immunity, you'll find it easier to stay healthy. Be honest with yourself about whether your eating and health habits prevent you from achieving that balance and set you up for all-out, exhausting wars against bacteria, viruses, cancer cells, and manmade toxins. Think about health habits that could help you develop and maintain robust immunity:

- eating well
- exercising adequately
- resting and sleeping adequately
- managing stress
- practicing good hygiene
- not smoking or vaping
- limiting alcohol and sugar consumption
- eating fermented foods/getting probiotics into your gut
- getting vaccinations recommended by your physician
- getting enough vitamin D/exposure to sunlight

As you consider building your immunity, remember that every warrior needs rest and restoration. Your immune system can be the home base from which rare wars are waged—if you're willing to change the story of your health and alter your health habits.

If you're doing your best to support your immune system but continue getting sick, consult your doctor—but also, consider consulting your hidden wisdom to learn more, let go of any energies that are contributing to your poor immunity, and bring in any energies that might support it. If you choose to do this, you can write about your experience here and consider setting a goal to help you attain or maintain robust immunity—here or earlier, when you were prompted to set a goal regarding your health.

The hidden-wisdom technique I used to help me learn more about my low immunity—and what I experienced when using it: _____

_____

_____

_____

_____

Keeping in mind the need for accountability, I'm setting this specific, achievable goal for making a change so I experience better immunity in the future: _____

_____

_____

_____

I achieved my goal: Yes No (Circle one)

Any notes on what helped or hindered me in trying to reach my goal: _____

_____

_____

_____

Using a hidden-wisdom technique, you can let go of any energies that are contributing to your poor immunity and bring in any energies that might support it.

Dance for Health, Dance for Healing

Dancing has many health benefits, from potentially preventing dementia to improving balance—and of course, it is a form of healthy aerobic exercise. It can even improve mood, so you might want to dance when you're feeling anxious, frustrated, angry, or sad. Dance for health, by all means. But you might also dance to gain insights and energy for healing so you can write a new story about yourself, your body, and your health.

Hidden-Wisdom Technique: Dancing for Insights

Dancing can help you get in touch with wisdom hidden in your unconscious. You might try to dance your battles with fatigue or with migraine headaches, simply putting on music that makes you want to move your body and intending to learn from your body's wisdom as you express yourself through dance. Allow your wise inner healer to speak to you as you sway and turn and you might experience certain words coming to mind, or images that are symbols with meanings worth exploring.

Once, I realized that dancing to the music of my youth could somehow help me work differently with the theme of constriction that had been influencing my health and my life for too long. I played some songs from the late 1950s, the kind I heard at parties when I was in high school and college, songs like Jerry Butler's "Your Precious Love" and Ritchie Valens' "La Bamba" that reminded me of love, yearning, and feeling free. I felt slightly awkward at first. Then I told myself, *Just dance. See what happens.*

As I moved, I mentally played with metaphors of constriction, rigidity, and imbalance. I listened to the wisdom of my body and my unconscious and recognized my desire to move toward expansiveness, flexibility, and balance in my body and in my life.

The experience reminded me that we can get locked into old patterns and automatically tell ourselves, *Oh, I can't do that anymore.* Dancing to music of the past can remind us of who we once were, of forgotten beliefs that we can bring back into our lives today and old ideas we need to discard.

Maybe you need to let yourself be a little awkward and hesitant as you discover how rigidity gets in the way of experiencing your body pleasurably. Maybe your dancing will show you that it is time to reclaim your ability to move with confidence despite any challenges and health issues you might have.

You might begin to dance away stories such as, *I need to be cautious—I can't trust myself and take risks.* You might discover that balance is something that returns when you let go of your fear of turning quickly to face a new direction. Your hidden wisdom can speak to you through your body.

Metaphors suggest themselves when you let go of your mind's constant need to tell you, *Be afraid* and *Go with what you know* or *Don't step out of your comfort zone.* As you dance, pay attention to what hidden wisdom arises.

When I danced to learn more about my health story or one of its chapters, I learned and experienced this: _____

_____

_____

_____

_____

_____

_____

You can not only dance your fatigue or dance your migraines, you can dance your job or your relationship with Spirit. You can dance your feelings, such as your anger or jealousy. Use your imagination to decide what you want to dance.

The Truth About Healing

As a clinical psychologist and Jungian analyst, I have worked with people facing a dire diagnosis, who were aware that no matter what they did to battle their disease, there was a strong chance that they would not survive. Most of us spend much of life in denial of our mortality, but then, suddenly, something will happen that awakens us to our vulnerability and the limitations of what we can control. A few years ago, I had triple bypass surgery, and less than a year later, I was treated for advancing prostate cancer. While I can do a lot using Western medicine to treat my health challenges, my study of shamanism and shamanic practices, which I began in earnest when I turned 60, helped me to understand that many people have a limited idea of what *healing* means. Too few recognize that they have a wise inner self that can help them achieve it.

As you think about your life, you might want to ponder what healing means to you and what, if anything, you would like to heal. For example, you might have physical ailments, old hurts that still sting, or a way of operating in the world that is not constructive or healthy that you would like to heal.

To me, healing would mean I could heal the following: _____

_____

_____

_____

_____

_____

If I were to experience this healing, my life would look like this (Note that you can write or draw your answer):

You might not experience a complete healing of something at the physical level, but a new perspective on health, illness, and mortality may both be possible and healing for you. You might also find that whatever you're suffering from or struggling with, whatever needs healing, can be improved, perhaps far more than you think it could. Regardless of what is happening with you that you would like to heal, resolving unfinished business with others or with Source might help you experience healing that you find valuable. You might find yourself developing a sense of calm, acceptance, and equanimity despite any challenges you face.

A new perspective on health, illness, and mortality may both be possible and healing for you.

Four Levels of Awareness Regarding Health and Healing

If you're not sure what healing can encompass, you might find it helpful to learn about the perspective found in Peruvian shamanism. Peruvian shamans, or healers, speak of four spirit animals or power animals associated with a medicine wheel used for healing. The snake is associated with the first point on the wheel, the south. This creature sheds its skin and experiences the world literally—in the simplest way. At the serpent level of awareness, everything is as it seems: Cancer is a disease in which cells that need to die remain alive and form tumors that spread. Eventually, if the growth is not arrested, the cancer cells cause death. There's no denying this harsh reality. But at the emotional or mental/emotional level of perception, associated with the west and the jaguar, cancer is an experience that makes us face our fears, including our fear of death but also perhaps our fear of not living a life that we find purposeful. At this perceptual level, we choose what meanings to make from our experiences.

How do we coexist with cancer once it comes, unbidden? Even if it goes into remission or is cured, how do we live with the energetic residue that it leaves and not get caught in worry that it will return? I've asked myself these questions. While cancer is a powerful force, those affected by it also have power—the power to choose how they will face and fight this frightening disease. In her book *Breast Cancer,* Patricia Greer, who was not only my wife but a gifted Jungian analyst, said that the most meaningful stand she took in writing a new story of her experience of cancer was to use this crisis as an opportunity to plant the seeds of spiritual and psychological growth. She pointed out that while we might work diligently to establish order, life is messy and inconvenient, and at times, "chaos may be exactly what is needed." Even in the best-tended garden, things that grow from below during the night can burst through, disrupting the planned pattern. She mused, is the point of a garden to organize or to ensoul?

To explain how her spiritual and psychological growth came about, Pat described images that came to her, some of them through dreams, that gave her the ability to understand and honor what was interior and secret, unknown to her conscious mind. Her belief was that in accessing and working with images that reveal hidden truths, we allow our inner treasure to spill forth. Cancer revealed the existence of encrusted habits she needed to discard so that new possibilities could emerge.

What Pat expressed could be described as seeing her life from the perspective of the hummingbird, associated with the north—and the third point on the Peruvian shamanic medicine wheel. The hummingbird takes a mythic, seemingly impossible journey of migration each year: from North America to South America, fueling itself for what seems an impossibly long flight and continuing on until it reaches its winter habitat and recharges. At the hummingbird level of perception, you see any life challenge you're facing, including a cancer diagnosis, as an invitation to take a mythic journey of change that will bring you to a much better place. Then, you might even see your journey as a spiritual one: You might see it from the level of the spiritual, as the eagle associated with the east. At this level, you can incorporate all the perspectives I've discussed so far and accept the mystery, the not knowing about what the future holds for you. You can deal with your challenges in practical ways, tame your fears and work with your emotions to strengthen yourself, see yourself as being on a mythic journey, and awaken your potential to rise above your fear and stories to experience yourself as a spiritual being with an eternal nature.

Do you see how healing from these different perspectives might look different from ridding your body completely of all disease and ailments, overcoming all your emotional and psychological challenges, and being cured?

The perspective of eagle is easier to experience by using techniques for quieting the activity of the mind enough to allow your wise inner self to show you who you are beyond your body, name, achievements, and relationships to others. I believe that deep down, you know that you're here on earth in this lifetime to do more than just live. You have much more to offer the world than simply existing. Accessing hidden wisdom can help you experience healing, but you must be willing to let go of your idea of exactly what that healing looks like.

By releasing old resentments, hurts, fears, and anger, you can find the lessons in your past suffering and begin to change your patterns. And as you learn to think differently about yourself and what happens to you, your problems and what you have suffered are likely to become relativized. You'll be able to focus more on your strengths than on your mistakes or on sad events that you experienced or are experiencing.

Losses are a part of life, and in the next chapter, you'll use hidden-wisdom techniques to help you contemplate endings, including the ending of your own life—which I hope is a long way off. Reflecting on the life you would've liked to have lived can help you break out of a robotic way of living and keep you from falling back into old patterns you wanted to discard. So while thinking about death might be unsettling, I strongly encourage you to try the exercises in the next chapter and see if they don't have value for you.

Chapter 15
Contemplating Your Life and Your Mortality

If the story of your life were to be told many years from now, how would the story end? Would it wrap up with you dying peacefully in your sleep, at an advanced age? Would your last years not only be healthy but filled with loving friends and family, excitement, and a sense of purpose? Would you have no remorse about the choices you made? As you look at the story of your life right now, I hope you are on the path to the ending you would like to experience.

In ancient times, aging poets in Japan would craft a death poem in acknowledgment that their time on earth was coming to an end and as a reflection on the life they had lived. It's said that when the Japanese poet Matsuo Basho was getting on in years, he was asked if he had written his death poem yet, and he responded that every poem he had ever written had been his death poem. In other words, his life's work was shaped by his awareness that we should live as if our lives might end at any moment—with no regrets and no sleepwalking through life.

According to lore, nineteenth-century Oglala Chief Low Dog said just before he led his troops into battle, "Today is a good day to die." Of course, it's uncomfortable to think about the fact that we might die, but we all will someday—something I'm very aware of because I'm in my eighties and have health issues. To me, "today is a good day to die" means that I live each day according to my values and priorities so that if it were to be my last day, I would be glad that I had spent it as I had.

While there is the death of the body, there's also a walking death of living according to old, stale habits. Refusing to replace them with more satisfying ones can make us feel even more melancholy than if we faced the truth about the way we are living, letting some things in our life die and making way for new things to grow. The energy of endings can help you to let go of things that need to die to make room for things that need to be born and grow.

Letting things die can be very difficult. Who will you be if you let go? What aspect of yourself might have to die? For example, as people grow older, they may have to let their homeowner self die so they can move into assisted living. At retirement, the sense of yourself as contributing to the world through working at a paid job might have to die. Letting go of being a parent of a child living in your home, who moves away to attend college or live in their first apartment, is a sort of death, too.

It can be difficult to accept that life brings changes you can't always control or even influence in any significant way. Even so, using hidden-wisdom techniques to consciously work with the energy of endings helps you to let go of what needs to be released.

Death and endings help us to better appreciate what we have and to commit to living more consciously and loving more deeply. If you work with the energy of endings, you may find it easier to accept the uncertainties of life and even the losses that might otherwise devastate you.

Whether you have just lost someone, or are about to, or are dealing with your own fear of your time in this life running out, or you sense there is something big that you need to let go of that you are clinging to, I hope you'll open to the possibility of working with the energy of endings, which can teach you about death. It might help you better appreciate the preciousness of every moment and open to the possibility of new beginnings. I feel that the gifts that come from dialoguing with the energy of endings are far too valuable for us to run from the prospect of something that sounds a little frightening.

When you're using a hidden-wisdom technique with the intention of meeting, interacting with, and learning from the energy of endings, your unconscious mind might represent death to you in an unexpected way. I've had a client encounter it as a faceless bureaucrat seated in an old-fashioned, abandoned schoolroom. Another client saw it as a magnificent and wise cobra. One of my clients said, "During a journey to meet death, I realized that death is an aspect of Source and that it is a very brightly illumined, inviting space. By the end of the journey, I felt that death and life are the same." Others have said they felt stronger and renewed after encountering and working with the energy of endings.

If you choose to use a hidden-wisdom technique to work with this energy to deal with an ending in your life, or to learn about what you need to let die, you can write or draw about your experience here.

My experience using a hidden-wisdom technique to work with the energy of endings was this:

Back to Basho

While thinking about death of the body can make you feel sad and scared, it can also help you to become aware of any choices you have made that have led to dissatisfaction, purposelessness, or perhaps a sense of numbness. You might want to contemplate your own death in a way that can be a little unsettling but ultimately rewarding: You can write a death poem, like Basho was asked about. I prefer to call it a life poem, and I suggest writing two versions:

- Your life poem of the life you have lived so far
- Your life poem of the life you would like to have lived, written as if you were at the end of your life, looking back

While writing a life poem is similar to identifying your story up to this point and writing a new one, which you've done more than once, this exercise using poetry instead of prose might yield valuable, fresh insights from your hidden wisdom.

Writing the poem of your life might yield valuable, fresh insights from your hidden wisdom.

In writing a poem about the life you have lived so far, you can make it free-form, or have it rhyme, or simply make it a beautiful and even poetic eulogy. Keep in mind that you still have time to make changes in the poem of the life you have lived, and as you write, consider whether there's a new way to think about any events that caused sorrow or regret.

The poem of my life so far is: _____

_____

_____

_____

_____

_____

_____

_____

_____

_____

_____

_____

_____

_____

_____

_____

_____

What Are You Willing to Let Go Of?

This section is especially for those of you who are getting older. You might be thinking about letting go of physical objects and possibly giving your time to others in service—and giving away some money rather than holding onto all of it. However, if you're still in the building up stage of your life rather than the letting go stage, you still might find some value in reading and working with this section, especially if you tend to hang onto possessions long after you stopped valuing them.

There's a legend that when Alexander the Great lay dying at the age of thirty-two, he made three last requests: for his doctors to carry his coffin, for gold and silver from his treasury to be spread over the road during the procession to his grave, and for his hands be positioned to hang over his coffin's sides. The idea was to show that even the best doctors might not be able to save us, we can't take our wealth with us, and we arrive in this world empty-handed and leave the same way.

When thinking about any treasures you have held onto, you might want to identify what you're willing to let go of and what you're not. It's possible to retain the fond memories of how you acquired and enjoyed them yet give them away. You can think about who would appreciate having your treasures after you're gone. You might want to let go of any possessions that remind you of what you meant to do or become someday but didn't. If you're willing to give up certain items but not others, consider writing about it here.

If there's something (or things) I am willing to let go of after all these years, it's this: _____

_____

_____

_____

I am ready to let go of these items because: _____

_____

_____

_____

If there's something (or things) I am not willing to let go of, even after all these years, it's this:

_____

_____

_____

_____

I am not ready to let go because: _____

_____

_____

_____

_____

It might be time to begin shifting your attention from building up security to creating a sense of purpose or, perhaps, adventure or connection, even if it means sacrificing some time, money, or possessions. You want to be sure that the work it takes to build up security will have been worth it when you look back at the end of your life and that you feel comfortable with the amount of time or money you gave away.

What would you like to experience in the future that your focus on security might be preventing you from experiencing? _____

_____

_____

_____

_____

Perhaps, too, you'd like to write a poem reflecting on the stage of life you're in—acknowledging what you're experiencing. As I am getting older, I'm no longer trying to accumulate things, such as possessions. Instead, I'm trying to shed what I don't need, including old behavioral patterns that no longer work for me, and focus on my priorities. I wrote the following poem about this shift:

Eternity

Not forever

is everything

Nothing is forever

Accumulation isn't

essence is

things aren't

patterns are—

Or are they?

If you would like to write about the stage of life you're in or are entering, exploring one or more of its themes, you might do so here. I find that the process of writing free-form poetry helps me gain insight into my hidden beliefs, bringing them into my consciousness. Drawing might do the same for you.

My poem or drawing about my current stage of life or the one I am entering:

When You Have Unfinished Business with Someone

If you were to take stock of your life, you might find you're uncomfortable with the amount of unfinished business you have with someone—or with more than one person. Maybe you meant to clear the air, but something always stopped you or you moved on too quickly, figuring that the conflict between you and someone else was no big deal. Reflecting on unfinished business can help you to take actions that will tie up loose ends, provide closure, and possibly help you and others to heal. You might discover that both you and the other person wronged each other. You might decide that it's best to accept that each of you has a point of view that is only going to change a small amount. Rather than decide how much you are at fault versus how much the other person is, you can choose to let go of the idea of fault and blame so that you can clear the air and repair the relationship.

You might want to resolve unfinished business even if it doesn't involve a conflict but something else, such as not expressing gratitude or love. I did this years ago, when my father was admitted to the hospital with a life-threatening condition. When I visited him at his bedside, I told him, "I love you, Dad." I hadn't said that to my father very often, even when I was a child. Men and boys growing up in the postwar Midwest often avoided sentimentality, and Dad and I conformed to that social norm. Now seemed a good time to make sure I affirmed what he surely knew but I rarely expressed.

"People throw that term around a lot, Carl," my father replied.

I paused, but then I pressed on. "That may be true, but still … I love you."

He seemed uncomfortable, but then he said quietly, "I love you, too."

My dad recovered from that health scare, but in the years that followed, until he passed away, he told the people he cared about *I love you* more often. Maybe my choice to break the old rules about what a father and son say to each other had loosened up something in him.

St. Francis is said to have been asked while he was working in his garden, "If you knew you were going to die tomorrow, what would you do?" His answer: "Keep working in my garden." Whatever your garden, however, you occupy your time, you might want to think about what you have and haven't done to resolve any unfinished business so that you feel you have no regrets. Consider answering the following questions.

Is there something you wish you'd said to a loved one but somehow never did, and if so, what stopped you? _____

_____

_____

_____

Have you been fully present for people in the ways you would want them to be present for you, and if not, what stopped you? _____

_____

_____

_____

Is there someone you have wronged that you have not yet asked forgiveness from? Circle one: Yes No

If so, would you like to clear the air with that person? Circle one: Yes No

If you would like to clear the air with that person, how could you do so? _____

_____

_____

_____

You might also try to track down the person you wronged to express regret and apologize. However, unfinished business with others may be something you have to resolve within yourself. That can be particularly true if the person with whom you would like to experience closure or resolution rebuffs your outreach to have a conversation or they ignore your letter or phone call to them.

If it would be impossible to get in touch with the person you wronged so that you could clear the air, you might try to think of an act of selflessness and kindness you could perform for someone else and do it with the intention of making up for the hurtful actions you took toward a person in your past.

Another option is to perform a ritual or an act that expresses atonement or forgiveness—or both. You can energetically release anger, guilt, resentment, sorrow or any combination of these. You might also release your need to be right, your need to have the last word, or your need to save face. For example, if you can't say to someone, *I'm sorry I spoke hurtful words to you* because the person is deceased or no longer in your life, you might use the following ritual to help you let go of stale energies that are preventing you from feeling a sense of closure and peace. You could use it to forgive someone in the sense that forgiveness would mean releasing any energy or emotions around what happened so that they no longer weigh you down.

Exercise: Ritual to Let It Go

A ritual outdoors or at an open window can help you to release whatever you want to let go of. You can rid yourself of the feeling of having unfinished business. You might say aloud or silently *I release my anger at this person* or *I release my need to get my adult son to see things my way* or something similar. You might release your guilt, regret, or anxiety. Then you can let the wind carry away your words and the energy of your feelings. As you do so, imagine the wind taking whatever it is that you've held onto for too long and dispersing it as it travels over land and water, far away from you. Alternatively, you might use the Ritual for Energy-Releasing and Energy-Absorbing exercise, which will have you working with water or fire. You'll find that exercise in Chapter 12: Resilience When Presented with Life's Suddenlies.

When you feel you've released what you need to let go of, pause and observe how you feel. Notice whether you feel relief, lightness, revitalization, emptiness, a sense that you're holding space for something new to come in, or anything else. Then, you can fill in the following.

My experience with the letting go ritual and how I felt about it:_____

_____

_____

_____

_____

If you have unfinished business and choose to use these exercises or a hidden-wisdom technique to help you deal with what feels unresolved, you can write about your experience here.

My thoughts on unfinished business of mine and anything I learned from using a hidden-wisdom technique for gaining insights and energy for resolving that unfinished business:

_____

_____

_____

_____

_____

_____

_____

_____

_____

You might also want to set a goal related to resolving unfinished business.

My goal for making a change regarding unfinished business with others is: _____

_____

_____

✔ **Did you accomplish your goal(s), and if so, what helped?** _____

_____

_____

If you did not accomplish your goal(s), why do you think that is? _____

_____

_____

You might want to resolve unfinished business even if it doesn't involve a conflict with others.

Your Bucket List

You've done a lot of work to identify what to bring into your life—new habits, more of a certain type of archetypal energy, and so on. Considering that you have limited time on this earth, think about what else you'd like to bring into your life—such as certain experiences.

Many people have a bucket list as part of their story about what they want to experience in this lifetime. You might want to write a bucket list or tidy up the one you have because it no longer reflects your values and deepest desires. Too often, we don't update our story or goals, only to find ourselves feeling inadequate or embarrassed because we haven't accomplished what we set out to do. Examining your bucket list might free up energy currently spent feeling guilty or ashamed and allow you to let go of those feelings. Make way for a consciously created bucket list that has meaning for you.

Maybe the thought of having a particular experience no longer excites you as it once did. Your guilt, frustration, or embarrassment at seeing what's been lingering on your list for years might be telling you that it's time to dream different dreams. For example, maybe you felt you had to do something to prove yourself to others. Impressing other people or getting their approval might not appeal to you as it once did. It's okay not to travel to the land of your ancestors just because your family always felt that's an important thing to do. If you don't feel the same way, let go of that dream. Perhaps you aspire instead to travel someplace where you can swim with dolphins or meet people from a completely different culture from your own.

Maybe your bucket list doesn't have any big, dramatic experiences on it. It could consist only of activities you're already doing and enjoying—maybe what you most desire is to continue to spend time with friends and family, doing creative writing, volunteering in your community, and so on.

Release the weight of having your bucket list heavy with other people's expectations of you and notice how much lighter you feel.

What's on my bucket list: _____

_____

_____

_____

_____

What, if anything, I don't want to be on my bucket list anymore: _____

_____

_____

_____

Keep in mind, too, that the *form* of the experience you told yourself you ought to have someday doesn't have to stay the same. You might decide to cross off *write a novel* and instead choose *write my life story and turn it into a book*. Maybe you no longer want *I will marry again* on your list and will replace that with *I will enjoy life with my new romantic partner regardless of whether I marry someday*. As you go down your list reading each item, listen to your heart. What still inspires you, and what makes you feel dispirited because you believed you ought to have made it happen by now? Explore whether you want to let go of that goal or change it to be more inspiring for you.

Tidying up your bucket list, or creating one for the first time, can be a good exercise in becoming more conscious of what you want to experience and why—and what dreams you are ready to release because you have new aspirations now. If you're spending your time doing what makes you feel a sense of vitality, happiness, and well-being, is there really anything you haven't yet done that generates a feeling of joy and anticipation when you think about it? If there is, that's what you should place it at the top of your bucket list. And don't just leave it there: Find a way today to start making it happen.

What I'd like to add to or prioritize on my bucket list: _____

_____

_____

_____

_____

What I can do today to make progress toward achieving my bucket list goals: _____

_____

_____

_____

_____

Keeping in mind the need for accountability, I'm setting this specific, achievable goal for doing something on my bucket list: _____

_____

_____

I achieved my goal: Yes No (Circle one)

Any notes on what helped or hindered me in trying to reach my goal: _____

_____

_____

_____

_____

Many people have a bucket list as part of their story about what they want to experience in this lifetime.

The Poem of the Life You Would Like to Have Lived

Earlier, you wrote the poem of the life you've lived until now. As I said, you might want to write a second poem: the poem of the life you wish to have lived, written as your future self at the end of your life, looking back. Write it as a poem, a eulogy, an obituary, or something else—whatever feels right to you.

As you do this, it's important to consider what to let go of and what to bring in so that the poem will indeed reflect the life you wished to have lived.

Once again, consider whether there's a new way to think about events that caused sorrow or regret—whether those are events you've already experienced or ones you suspect you'll experience.

The poem of the life I will have wished to have lived: _____

_____

_____

_____

_____

_____

_____

_____

_____

_____

If life seems dull and without any sense of the mystical, perhaps you can take advantage of opportunities to feed your hunger for poetry and beauty. You can imagine what might your life be like someday because of any new choices you make now. You can imagine, too, what will bring a smile to your face as you reflect on it. What would you like to be able to say about awe-inspiring moments? You might want to think about the beauty in life that has inspired a sense of awe and wonder in you. As you recall these exquisite moments, you can think about what you could do to experience more of them, and use that to inform the poem of your life that you write from the perspective of your future self, who has lived the life you hope to have lived.

Notes on mystical, exquisite, awe-inspiring moments I've had that can help me recognize how to experience more of these: _____

_____

_____

_____

_____

You might want to reread your two different life poems and ask yourself the following.

What can I do in the time I have left to shift from the poem about the life I've lived so far to the poem about the life I wish that I will have lived? _____

_____

_____

_____

_____

What, if any, obstacles or challenges are there to living the life I wish I will have lived? _____

_____

_____

_____

_____

_____

Now that I have done the work of this workbook, what are some ways I can deal with obstacles and challenges and find moments of joy and awe regardless? _____

_____

_____

_____

_____

_____

If there are things you feel you need to do to be able to reflect on your life some day and have it match your poem of the life you would've liked to live, you might want to set some new goals for yourself. You'll find space in the back of the book to do that.

Applying insights to your everyday life and at least making changes around the margins will help you bring a new story to life. Remember, one change leads to another. Your progress may be slow, but at least you'll be moving forward into a more satisfying life. And who knows? Using the hidden-wisdom techniques, you may achieve a breakthrough or two that vaults you forward.

Again, you can always write a new story and bring it to life. If you want more joy and more time with people you love, never be afraid to ask yourself whether you're on the path to making that happen—because if the answer is no, you now have tools and techniques for transformation. I congratulate you for doing all the work you've done in this workbook to bring about changes. Within you is much hidden wisdom and the power to change unseen influences affecting you. May you achieve the life you long to live.

Appendix
Additional Goals

Here, you can record any extra goals you came up with and didn't have room to record in the workbook. Keep in mind what you've learned about overcoming obstacles, establishing new habits, and holding yourself accountable, including syncing your goals to your calendar and having check-in points. You might want to record here the dates by which you hope to have achieved your goal—and mark those dates, and check-in dates, on your calendar.

Keeping in mind the need for accountability, I'm setting this specific, achievable goal:

_____

_____

_____

_____

I achieved my goal: Yes No (Circle one)

Any notes on what helped or hindered me in trying to reach my goal: _____

_____

_____

_____

_____

Keeping in mind the need for accountability, I'm setting this specific, achievable goal:

_____

_____

_____

_____

I achieved my goal: Yes No (Circle one)

Any notes on what helped or hindered me in trying to reach my goal: _____

_____

_____

_____

_____

Keeping in mind the need for accountability, I'm setting this specific, achievable goal: _____

_____

_____

_____

_____

I achieved my goal: Yes No (Circle one)

Any notes on what helped or hindered me in trying to reach my goal: _____

_____

_____

_____

_____